KALEIDOSCOPE

Also by Margaret Jones Bolsterli

The Early Community at Bedford Park

Vinegar Pie and Chicken Bread

Born in the Delta

A Remembrance of Eden

During Wind and Rain

Things You Need to Hear

Kaleidoscope

*Redrawing an
American Family Tree*

Margaret Jones Bolsterli

The University of Arkansas Press
Fayetteville
2015

ISBN: 978-1-55728-815-8
e-ISBN-13: 978-1-61075-562-7

19   18   17   16   15   5   4   3   2   1

Designed by Liz Lester

☉ The paper used in this publication meets the minimum requirements
of the American National Standard for Permanence of Paper for Printed
Library Materials Z39.48–1984.

LIBRARY OF CONGRESS CONTROL NUMBER: 2014958342

For Will Franklin,
Barbara Campbell Staples, Lorna Campbell,
and the memory of the late Albert Campbell Jr.

Time present and time past
Are both perhaps present in time future,
And time future contained in time past.
If all time is eternally present
All time is unredeemable.
What might have been is an abstraction
Remaining a perpetual possibility
Only in a world of speculation.
What might have been and what has been
Point to one end, which is always present.
Footfalls echo in the memory
Down the passage which we did not take
Towards the door we never opened
Into the rose-garden. My words echo
Thus, in your mind.

    But to what purpose
Disturbing the dust on a bowl of rose-leaves
I do not know.

    Other echoes
Inhabit the garden. Shall we follow?

—from *Burnt Norton*, T. S. ELIOT

CONTENTS

I suspect that there are few white southerners, especially older ones, who have not wondered at some time in their lives whether there might be a drop or two of African blood from some unexplained but imaginable source coursing through family veins. That passing thought used to be too terrible to contemplate for long; but it was there, in the collective consciousness, brought on, perhaps, by a glance in one's own mirror or at a relative's head of crisp, curly hair or a complexion that tans darker in summer than Scotch Irish or English or German or French skin is supposed to. Sometimes, according to some of the people who helped me with this project, these traits might be mentioned in a teasing way by other children and occasionally in downright accusations that registered but were never taken seriously.

This possibility, that miscegenation might have occurred in one's family in the span of almost four hundred years during which whites and blacks have been living close together in the United States, hovering in the background of the southern imagination, was easy to ignore until recently. Americans, as we know, have always been masters of self-reinvention. Traditionally, when we have pulled up stakes and "gone west" to begin a new life, the records of the old one could be left behind and we could become, to our new neighbors and to the government, who and what we claimed to be. Nobody would know the difference. But when the introduction of the Internet gave easy access to public records that had previously been practically inaccessible, this ignorance ended. Public records are now truly public and accessible to anyone with a computer. We have all been "outed" where race is concerned.

So far, my family is the only one of my acquaintance where the suspicions have proved true, but I doubt that it will be the last. As one friend said on hearing it, "If it could happen in your family, it could have happened in anybody's and probably did." Another had a

DNA test done immediately. "Just out of curiosity," he said. And, of course, many members of my own family, including me, had DNA tests done, just to make sure our newly discovered history could be true. (Mine showed approximately 6 percent African ancestry, from West Africa, specifically: Mali, 3 percent; Senegal, 1 percent; and [strangely, because most Africans came to America from West Africa] the Bantu tribe in Southeastern Africa, 2 percent, which, I suppose puts my ancestors in the same tribe that produced Bishop Desmond Tutu!) So it is obvious that although the significance of racial origin in the United States is changing in the twenty-first century, when we have an African American president and African Americans are successful in all other professions as well, it is still very much a matter of interest.

There are two stories in this book. One concerns my surprise and change in vision brought about by learning of my mother's descent from a slave-holding, free-colored pioneer family near Vicksburg, some of whom, when driven out of Mississippi in 1859, simply crossed the Mississippi River and passed into the white world, to be joined in about 1875 by my great-grandmother and grandfather. All, categorized "M" for mulatto in the US census while living in Mississippi, were "W" for white when the census takers came around in Arkansas for the 1860 and 1880 counts.

The other story is about what could be gleaned from public records about the lives of my newly found relatives, starting with my great-great-grandfather Jordan Chavis's service in the War of 1812, through his first appearance in the tax records in Mississippi in 1829 and his rise to prosperity as a frontier farmer, his fortunes through the Civil War and its aftermath, until his death in 1873 and the final loss of the family's land in 1882, sold at the courthouse door in Vicksburg to settle his grandson's debts. I include what could be learned about his children, one of whom moved his family to Illinois in 1857, then returned to Mississippi in 1871 and was elected to serve in the 1874 Reconstruction legislature. Some of his descendants identify themselves as African Americans; some have passed into the white world.

As I see it, our forebears were denied their rights because of color; and we, the succeeding generations, by being denied the stories of their lives and achievements, have been deprived of a significant part of our history. Although I am fully aware of the reasons behind the silence about them, I believe that hearing their stories would have influenced us and others with similar heritage to look at racial matters in a different light. Because when I finally found out who my ancestors were and what their lives had been like, the pattern in the kaleidoscope through which I had always looked at my family was irreparably altered and, to modify slightly a line from William Butler Yeats's poem "Easter 1916," about a huge transformation in his vision, in my case also, "a terrible beauty *was* born."

I think that these stories, put together, add up to something else: an example in microcosm of the role that race has played in American society and the ways in which that role seems to be changing now at the speed of light. While this memoir and family history is neither an analysis of white identity in the United States nor even an organized examination of one family's experiences with it, I hope scholars in that nascent field of American studies will find it useful.

This is the third and final book I intend to write about my family. I plan to devote my remaining time to fiction, which cannot be any stranger than the truth I have told here. After all, as historians never tire of reminding me, I am a storyteller, not a historian. May it ever be so.

ACKNOWLEDGMENTS

I have had more help with research for this project than any writer has a right to expect. Through the magic of the Internet, I have been in contact with relatives both close and distant, including many that I never knew I had before this subject was handed to me in 2005 by my cousin, the late Albert Campbell Jr, his wife, Lorna, and his sister Barbara Staples in emails that introduced me to the existence of our long-dead ancestor Jordan Chavis. I will always be grateful, not only for the initial information that started the whole thing, but for their willing contribution of genealogical material they had collected and for their continued support over the many years it has taken me to complete the writing of the narrative their interest in genealogy led me to. They also contributed the photograph of Jerusha Chavis Cason, my great-grandmother, their great-great grandmother. Without these "Campbell cousins" this work would never even have been started.

Of equal importance with those contributions ranks their introduction to me of another, even more distant cousin, Will Franklin, whose help exceeds any expression of gratitude I can muster. At the time he met the Campbells through their common interest in the Chavis family on ancestry.com, Will had already done extensive genealogical research on the family and, in addition, had collected vast amounts of other material, including court claims that he donated to me for use in this work. He was always there to offer encouragement and advice on problems I encountered, from computer glitches to ways of finding things on the Internet, and at one point engaged a professional genealogist in South Carolina to track down information not available electronically. He solicited photographs from his genealogical network and worked on ancient photographs until the faces became clear enough to show resemblances to each other and to their descendants. He read the manuscript in progress and offered suggestions and encouragement.

The Campbell cousins started me on this project, but without Will Franklin's help I could not have completed it.

Will put me in contact with a historian in Mississippi, Jeff Giambrone, who agreed to work as my research assistant there for a month, tracking the Chavis family in tax records, deeds, newspaper articles, and any other sources we could think of in the archives at the Mississippi Department of Archives and History in Jackson and the Old Court House Museum in Vicksburg. I could not have asked for a better job of finding and organizing material!

When I finally made my way to Vicksburg, I was warmly welcomed by George Bolm, the director of the Old Court House Museum, and assisted with material on the Chavis family he had already pulled out for me.

Elizabeth Payne offered valuable suggestions and encouragement at several steps along the way and led me to Sue Moore, a historian of Mississippi who sent me useful information about the cluster of slave-holding, free-colored planters in Claiborne and Jefferson Counties.

Other cousins who offered information about family and/or photographs were Donna Preston, Kathy Lawrence, and Jennifer Sands Congleton.

I appreciated the opinions on the matter of racial significance offered by the following family members of the younger generation: Will Franklin, Eric Bolsterli, Melinda Holder, Robin Looney, Bill Lloyd, Donna Preston, Jerry Jones, Lorri Daniels, Jamie Daniels, Barbara Staples, and Sam Cason.

Eric Bolsterli, Hilary Harris, and Grif Stockley, as well as Will Franklin, read the manuscript carefully and offered good suggestions for its improvement, as did the anonymous readers provided by the University of Arkansas Press.

Beth Stockdell ably filled the generation gaps between me and the computer age.

As for the University of Arkansas Press, I take this occasion of their sixth publication of one of my books to thank the directors and staff, past and present, for the many years of our very satisfactory association. It has been an honor to say where my work about Arkansas was published.

As always, the constant encouragement given by Olivia Sordo kept the fire lit under this project from beginning to end. As she had for the other five books I have written in the last forty years, Olivia read and reread ad infinitum draft after draft and took part in endless conversations about the progress and ultimate completion of the enterprise, which she never doubted, as I sometimes did. My gratitude is boundless.

I thank all those who helped for their contributions, but I would like to say that the shaping of the narrative and the final interpretations are entirely mine.

CHAPTER I

The Kaleidoscope Turns

In 1991, I published a memoir, called *Born in the Delta,* about growing up in the Arkansas-Missippi Delta on a cotton farm that has belonged to my father's family since 1849. The subtitle was *Reflections on the Making of a Southern White Sensibility.* It would be hard to imagine a family whiter than we were: staunch white Anglo-Saxon Protestants in a straight line all the way back to Adam and Eve, who, of course, had been created in his own image by God.

And then sometime in 2005, out of the blue, I received an email from a cousin on my mother's side of the family informing me that he had good reason to believe that my maternal ancestors were mulattoes, free people of color residing in Mississippi before the Civil War. This cousin, Albert Campbell Jr., the grandson of my mother's sister, Mary Jerusha Cason Campbell, had taken early retirement because of poor health and, bored to death, had joined ancestry.com and turned to genealogy to pass the time. Of course I did not believe him but said I would be happy to look at whatever evidence he had found that led him to think it. How could this be true? The suggestion defied both imagination and reason.

When Albert and Lorna, his wife and partner in research, sent me their extensive, carefully organized notes and relevant family trees, I joined ancestry.com and got on the Internet to check things out for myself. Before this, I had never even heard the family name of our Mississippi forbears. It was Chavis. My mother's great-grandfather, who had died in December 1873 in Warren County, Mississippi, was named Jordan Chavis. As the Campbells had, I followed him back through the census records from Mississippi in 1870 to Murfreesboro, Tennessee, in 1820 and found that in all six censuses he is designated either "free colored" or, beginning in 1850, "M" for mulatto.

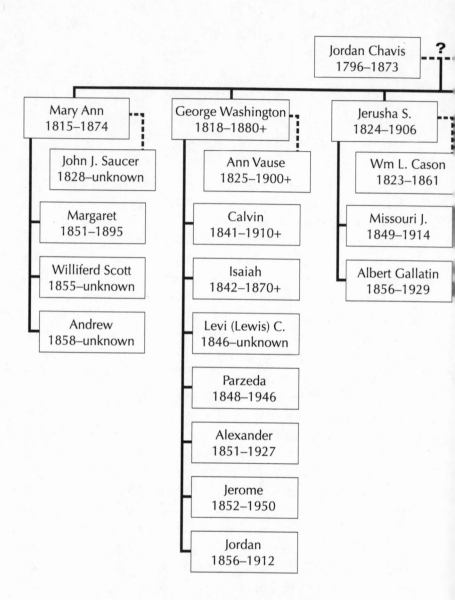

Jordan Chavis–Nancy Chavis (?)
Descendants Chart

Author's grandfather was Albert Gallatin Cason.

FIGURE 1. Jordan Chavis–Nancy Quick (?) Descendants Chart.

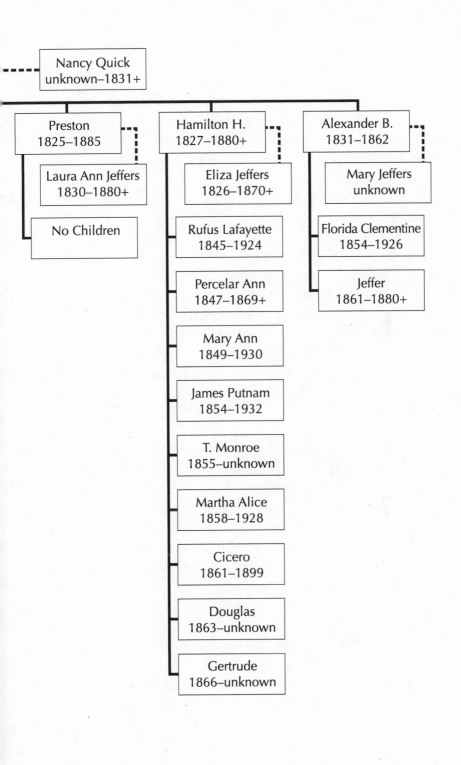

Still, even after looking at the evidence, I could not quite believe it. Neither could my two remaining siblings. This was a mind-boggling possibility. If true, how could we not have heard even a whisper about it? Surely our mother knew; she must have. There had never been mention of it in Cousin Albert's branch of the family, either. I got in touch with the descendants of one of Mother's brothers and they were as surprised and prone to denial as we were. Questions arose. My mother must have known, but had she told my father? They were both dead by then, as were all of their siblings. As I said, it would be hard to imagine a family *whiter* than ours. And yet . . .

Albert and Lorna Campbell put me in touch with a distant cousin they had met online through ancestry.com who was doing research on the same family, a man named Will Franklin, whose work settled the matter beyond all doubt. For, in addition to census records providing genealogical material, he had collected such things as transcripts of court records that included personal statements by Jordan Chavis and his son Preston affirming their positions as successful planters in Warren County, Mississippi, before, during, and after the Civil War and establishing their racial designation beyond question. Looking at the material he forwarded removed my doubts and encouraged me to believe that there might be more documentation available than I had at first feared there might be. Records get lost, ink fades, private houses as well as courthouses burn, especially during a civil war. Genealogy is a good place to begin, but a narrative needs records; after all, what would the Old Testament mean if we had only the "begats"? I needed all the information I could get to put flesh on the skeleton that ancestry.com provided and my cousins had collected and passed on to me.

But back to my story. Our farm, when I was growing up there in the 1930s, followed the plantation model of operation, with sharecroppers and tenant farmers providing the labor and my father and the bank he borrowed it from providing the capital. My paternal great-grandfather had bought this land in the 1840s, cleared it from virgin forest, and worked it with slaves until the Civil War. My grandfather, who fought as a Confederate foot soldier in many of the major battles of that misguided rebellion, walked home from North Carolina when Joseph E. Johnston surrendered in 1865 and took on the role of owner in 1872 at the death of his father. My own father stepped into the harness in 1905 when his father died. My oldest brother's turn came in 1957, and my nephew, his son, owns the place now. The house I grew up in was built on the spot where my father had grown up. I left that house in 1948 to go to college and after that returned only as a visitor, but I am absolutely certain that the seventeen years I spent there listening to stories about that family formed the patterns in my mind so indelibly that everything I have learned since is like a transparent overlay on a map that adds new details without obscuring the original, or a palimpsest, an ancient parchment on which no matter how much the text gets written over, fragments of the first writing remain, hidden but recoverable.

In *Born in the Delta* and a companion memoir, *During Wind and Rain*, I have written extensively about our life there in that "little house in the swamp." Until recently, I thought I knew all there was to know about my family and our situation and, furthermore, thought I had written all there was to write about us, them. By *us*, I mean my immediate family, my parents and my four brothers and a sister and aunt who were already in the house when I was born in 1931. By *them* I mean the ancestors on both sides of my father's family who had come there to the frontier from Tennessee and fought the forest with its snakes, bears, wolves, panthers, mosquitoes, diseases, and isolation to make a life for us. These forbears were still there with us all the time in stories told to entertain and parables meant to incite good behavior. There were even stories about the houses and relatives left behind in Tennessee when the family moved to Arkansas. Columbia, Tennessee, and the land around it was "the old country" in our family. It was a lost paradise where everything was shining and civilized; one or two of my aunts had been sent back there to school, since at that time none with more than one room was available where we lived, and returned with fresh stories to keep the myths alive. My father, Grover Cleveland Jones, nicknamed "Boss," was bitter until the day he died about not having been sent to school in Columbia himself. The peaches in Maury County, Tennessee, were lusher, and the mules bigger and stronger. It was, as my father would say proudly, "the mule capital of the world." And, indeed, driving to Columbia sometime about 1995 I passed a sign on the highway that still makes that claim. Every surviving stick of furniture and piece of chipped crockery that had come to Arkansas with these people and survived the 1927 flood was revered. My father shaved every morning staring into the same mirror his father and grandfather had stared into from young manhood to old age. The presence of these grandparents, aunts, uncles, and cousins long gone was as real to us as if they had just stepped off the front porch, climbed into a buggy, and disappeared in a cloud of dust. The stories about them were affirmed by tintypes, photographs, locks of hair, and old clothes in trunks where the important family papers were kept. The records of their births and deaths were carefully recorded in the family Bible. The books they read were still around, with their names signed on the flyleaves. These people seemed very real and it was made clear that it was up to us not to let them down by bad behavior and failures of one kind or another. Although ghosts by then, apparently they still had expectations.

My mother, Zena Cason, had come to that house to board in 1908 as the young teacher for the local one-room school, and she and Boss fell in love and married before the end of her first year. At the age of twenty-two, he was already head of the household consisting of himself and two sisters, one older and one younger. Mother had grown up on a smaller farm some fifty miles away, in Ashley County, in a house full of brothers and sisters. The few stories she brought to the table were mostly about her immediate family: her parents, brothers and sisters, and "Little Grandma," her father's mother who lived with them and had a hand in raising the children. It was this grandmother who taught refinement and encouraged the children to get as much education as they possibly could, influencing Mother and at least one of her sisters to work their way through a couple of years of college to earn teaching certificates.

There was a legend in the family that Mother's grandparents had owned a plantation in Mississippi so ravaged by Union troops during the Civil War that they had been forced to move into Vicksburg. Then one day some years after the war my adolescent grandfather was hanging around the railroad yard with the black teenager who had been his companion and minder (assigned to keep an eye on him during his childhood) when they got locked in a boxcar that was not opened until it arrived in Monticello, Arkansas. Young Albert Gallatin Cason, my grandfather, climbed down out of the boxcar, looked around, and liked what he saw so much that he wrote his mother, Jerusha Chavis Cason, to sell the land and come. Since the Yankees had burned everything else, the land was all they had left. Jerusha did as he advised and they bought a small farm near Fountain Hill in Ashley County. That was the story of the way the Cason family came to be in Arkansas. Jerusha, of course, was "Little Grandma." This is essentially all we ever heard about Mother's family before they left Mississippi. As a child I thought of that lost plantation as a mirror image of the one we were living on in the Delta. How right and yet how wrong that vision was, as I have come to learn. It lacked one very significant element.

I no longer believe that Albert got locked up in that railroad car by accident. I think he climbed into it because he knew where it was going and that was where he wanted to go. For it turns out that a family haven had already been established there in southeastern Arkansas by two of his uncles and an aunt who, with their families, had fled Mississippi in 1859 when the legislature, deciding to rid the state of free people of color, gave them the choice of either leaving or being sold into slavery. As for young Albert, the mid–1870s probably seemed as good a time for him and his mother to be leaving as 1859 had been for his mother's siblings. For, according to the opinion of whites, the Chavis family was on the wrong side of Reconstruction in 1875, caught in the bitter fight that led to the suppression of black suffrage in Mississippi that was not relieved until the passage of the Voting Rights Act of 1965.

In its simplest terms, this is the new picture that I was eventually able to put together: I am a descendant of Jerusha Chavis

Cason, one of the four children of a man named Jordan Chavis, who crossed the Mississippi River to Arkansas and passed, with their families, into the white world.

Another son, who had freed a slave woman and married her in 1840, had gone north in 1857, retaining his mulatto identity, where some of his descendants still identify themselves as African American and some have also passed into the white world. This son, George Washington, returned to Mississippi in 1871 and was elected to the Mississippi legislature in 1873, the much-reviled Reconstruction legislature. His son Calvin, as deputy sheriff of Warren County, witnessed the white mob's retaking of the sheriff's office in December 1874, the first step in removing elected black officials from office in Mississippi and the beginning of the infamous "Vicksburg Troubles."

If the bare facts of the simple view are surprising, the implications, as we will see later, are stunning.

If my mother knew stories about all this, as I am sure she must have, I wish she had related them to us, but there was never a whisper. When she was growing up in the 1890s there would still have been talk about it in the house because in a southern household at that time stories were told. Over and over. And in addition to those, there were surely tales about how her grandmother Jerusha and young Albert, my grandfather, and Jerusha's daughter Missouri, her husband, Osburn Jeffers, and their children also made the move some ten or twelve years later. The members of Jerusha's family, this second group of immigrants, were all designated "M" in the 1870 census in Mississippi and "W" in the 1880 census in Arkansas. Again, we never heard mention.

And what of the *pater familias*, Jordan Chavis and his other son, Preston, who remained in Mississippi? How did they survive the Civil War and its aftermath? Who were all these people who were suddenly somehow present in my consciousness but yet still absent? They were not even ghosts, as my father's people were; they could not exist in my imagination because I had no context for them. They were blank outlines in empty spaces, just unfamiliar names in unfamiliar places.

Confronting this new information was like looking at what I had thought was my family's history through a kaleidoscope: There is the picture and then a slight turn of the lens reshapes the familiar components into a new pattern, somehow the same but different. Because the picture of a Mississippi cotton plantation complete with slaves owned by free people of color is a different pattern. Growing up southern white does not prepare one to imagine a mulatto Scarlett in the "Big House" of your family's fantasies. And yet the only extant picture of my great-grandmother, Jerusha Chavis Cason, a tintype that turned up in Aunt Mary Campbell's trunk of important papers, shows her dressed richly enough to have been the mistress of Tara. It is a picture of Jerusha and her son Albert, my grandfather, made about 1862, judging from little Albert's size.

It occurred to me that our surprise must resemble that of people who learn that not only were their ancestors Jewish, but they were caught up in the Holocaust and survived. There are undeniable similarities between Mississippi in the nineteenth century and the Third Reich.

The more I thought about all this, the more obvious it became that the real story here is not about *us*. It's about *them*, the absent ones who were at the dinner table too, in my mother's mind and in our history and in our genes; we just didn't know it when we were listening to those stories about the *white* side of the family. They were in the stories Mother didn't tell. They were there in the tapestry of our lives as they were there in the fabric of our national life, about which we weren't being told the whole truth either.

We never doubted the courage and perseverance it took to go to the frontier and thrive as my father's white forebears had. As children, we had the lessons learned from that experience drilled into us at home and at school. But the qualities of their characters pale beside the courage and perseverance it must have taken for free people of color to go to the frontier and thrive and then years later to cross a river to another slave state and *secretly pass from one caste to another* in a matter of a few days to keep from being sold into slavery. Or the courage it took for my great uncle Washington, as he was called, to free the slave woman he loved, marry her, and then, *against the law*, return to Mississippi to live with her and raise a family.

A question we may well ponder is how our characters might have been formed differently if we had been brought up knowing about *their* trials. Another question worth thinking about is how common this experience may have been in one form or another. Because another persistent question is this: When the free people of color in southern states were told they had to leave wherever they were or be sold into slavery, where did they go?

How might the national character have been formed differently if stories like this one had been talked about at our dinner table and everywhere else? Of course, we know why they were not; the subject was too dangerous to touch until recently. Just how dangerous may be one of the things my recounting here helps define.

It seemed to me that I had an obligation to learn as much as I could about "them" in order to comprehend "our" story, so I decided to put together in this book everything my newly found cousins and I could find out about our lost relatives in Mississippi in an attempt to understand, as well as possible, who they were and how they lived.

Sometimes it takes a long time for them to be heard, but strange as it seems, silenced voices echo too.

CHAPTER 2

Jordan Chavis Establishes
Himself in Mississippi

If I had run across the following article from the June 21, 1861, *New York Times* or the original article it references in the *Vicksburg Whig*, I would have been interested in knowing more about Jordan Chavis even if he hadn't been my newly found great-great-grandfather.

No Prejudice Against Color

The Vicksburg Whig is in extacies over a free negro named Jordan Chavis, who has written a letter to the agent of the Confederate Loan, in which he states that he has long been a resident of the County, and had received a land-warrant for services in the War of 1812; but being too old for active service, he now desires to present a horse to a cavalry company, and he also authorizes the agent to draw upon him for $500, to be paid out of his next crop, for the use of the Confederacy. The respectful manner in which the Whig speaks of CHAVIS is a little remarkable, especially in view of the Dred Scott decision. The paragraph is headed "Patriotic Liberality of a Colored Man." There is no intimation that he is a "negro," or a "nigger," or even a "boy," but he is spoken of as a "real bonafide colored man, long well known in this community, who, by his correct and honest deportment, has gained the esteem of all who knew him." We doubt whether any "free nigger" who could not bring five hundred such substantial reasons for the respect of the Southern Confederacy as CHAVIS did, could get so high a eulogium from a Southern journal.[1]

Who could read this without wondering who this colored man was and how he had managed to reach a position of such generosity and confidence. Five hundred dollars was a considerable sum

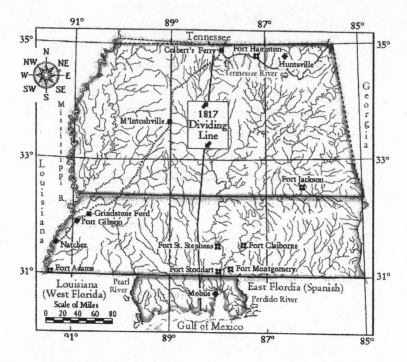

FIGURE 2. Territory of Mississippi, 1798–1817. *Courtesy TnGenWeb.*

in 1861; according to the US census, the average annual wage in Mississippi in 1860 was $338! Not to mention the value of the horse. Furthermore, the crop, since this is Vicksburg, Mississippi, would have had to be cotton, and therefore not to be harvested until August and later, a capricious expectation on which to base the promise of a donation in June because there is always a good chance that even if a substantial crop makes it to harvest, after the debts are paid for the costs to produce it, little or nothing will be left. The success of a crop depends on the weather, the absence of insects, the health of the labor force, the availability of credit, and other variables. His cotton could have been ankle high by June and promising, but too much or too little rain could ruin it before harvest time. How was he going to make this crop? Farming on this scale in that place and time required credit and the use of slave labor. Jordan Chavis was a colored man. Did he own land as a basis

FIGURE 3. Mississippi in 1828.
Courtesy Tom Paradise, PhD,
Cartographer.

for credit? If so, how did he get hold of it? Did he own slaves? If so, how many and when did he acquire them?

But the question that looms even larger than those regarding Chavis's ability to make this offer good when the time came is, of course, the question of why is he doing this at all. What color was he, anyway, if he was supporting the Confederacy? And what did that mean for the kind of life he and his family could lead? How free was a "free Negro" in Mississippi in the nineteenth century? It is worth noting that he was neither alone nor the first among his peers to show support for the Confederacy. A few weeks earlier, on May 6, 1861, the following bit appeared in the *Vicksburg Weekly Citizen:* "Henry Lee, a free man of color of this city has give $25 towards equipping the Sharpshooters."[2] The Sharpshooters was the name of a Vicksburg Confederate militia. And on June 24, the *Vicksburg Weekly Herald* reported, "Green Boles, a free negro of this city this morning stepped into the office of Col. Brooke, and sub-scribed $150 to the Confederate States loan, and said that in a few days he expected to receive another hundred dollars, which he also intended to invest in the same way."[3] Why were these free men of color doing this?

I ask the reader to bear with me as I try to answer these com-plicated questions in what, because of the elusive nature of the evidence, must be a digressive, convoluted account because there's not only the family story here but also one that ought to be fitted into the greater narrative of the making of the United States that we are still writing after all these years because of *its* elusive nature.

Fortunately, we can begin with information provided under oath by Jordan Chavis himself. In a petition to the government in 1871, requesting reimbursement for goods taken from him by the Union army in June 1863, shortly before the fall of Vicksburg, he makes a personal statement in which he tells that he is seventy-eight years of age and was born free in South Carolina. Although he gives other birthdates in various documents, this is the most probable, judging from other evidence.[4] (This claim, which was unsuccessful, will come into the story later as testimony to Chavis's account of his experiences as a Union sympathizer during the Civil War.) The year 1793 seems probable as his birth date, not only because he claims to be seventy-eight in this petition but because it also means that he would have been twenty-one when drafted, as he claimed, for service in 1814 in the War of 1812 in Murfreesboro, Tennessee, and also puts him in the correct age range to be the Jordan Chavis named to represent his presumed wife, Nancy Quick Chavis, in the disposition of property left her by her father, Aquilla Quick, in Marlboro County, South Carolina, on March 2, 1813.[5]

As for his having been born free, the Chavis family by this time had been free for over a hundred years, according to Paul Heinegg, whose massive study, *Free African Americans of North Carolina, Virginia, and South Carolina from the Colonial Period to about 1820,* is the benchmark of scholarship on free people of color in early America. He states, "In 1810 . . . the Chavis family, free since the seventeenth century, headed forty-one households containing forty-six persons in Virginia, 159 in North Carolina and twelve in South Carolina."[6] He further states, "Many free African Americans originated or moved to Surry County, Virginia, where their deeds, marriage bonds, and wills were recorded in the seventeenth and eighteenth centuries. Among them were the Chavis and Jeffrey families."[7]

In 1672, near Jamestown, a free woman named Elizabeth Chavis sued successfully for the freedom of her son Gibby Gibson under a recent Virginia law mandating that the children of a union between a slave and a free person would take the status of the mother.[8] Although the Gibsons do not show up again in this story about the Chavises, Elizabeth's other son, Hubbard, was the progenitor of a distinguished free-colored family that left Virginia and lived in North Carolina, South Carolina, and Warren County, Mississippi, on their way to Louisiana, becoming white on the journey somewhere between South Carolina and Mississippi. (As explanation for the "dark strain" in the Gibson family, a story was handed down that "four Gibson youths, children of the younger son of an English lord and a Gypsy maid," had sailed from England to Virginia in the seventeenth century!)[9]

Jordan is a Chavis family name passed down through the generations, also mentioned in 1775 in Wake County, North Carolina.

Many members of these free families were financially successful under the terms of the day. "The Bunch, Chavis and Gibson families owned slaves and acquired over a thousand acres of land on both sides of the Roanoke River in present-day Northampton and Halifax Counties, and the Chavis and Gowen families acquired over a thousand acres in Granville County."[10] It is thought that these were tri-racial families with some mixture of white, African American, and Indian blood who descended from some combination of white indentured servants, black slaves, and Indians. But whatever the mix, and whenever and however it took place, the result was enough to brand the Chavis family "free colored" until 1859, when two of Jordan's sons, Hamilton and Alexander, and a daughter, Mary Ann, with their families, crossed the Mississippi into Arkansas and became thereafter officially "white" in the US census. Sometime in the mid 1870s, Jordan's daughter Jerusha and her son Albert Gallatin Cason joined them. Jerusha, my great grandmother, and Albert, my grandfather, designated "M" for mulatto in Mississippi in the 1870 census, were "W" for white when the census taker came around in Arkansas in 1880.

Being "born free" in 1793 meant primarily that Jordan Chavis was not born a slave. Nobody owned his mother and, therefore, Jordan. But the very fact that it had to be stated signified a special category of "not white." His birthright was a qualified freedom in a tenuous in-between world of "free colored," which carried slightly different restrictions at different times and in different states. Generally speaking, he could own property and bear witness against a slave, but not against a white man, although a white man could sue or accuse him in a court of law. He could not vote in South Carolina, although he could in North Carolina and Tennessee until 1835, perhaps an asset to Jordan Chavis when he lived in Tennessee between 1813 and 1828 or so, although his name does not appear on the voter lists. As a free-colored person, he had to be able to prove at all times that he was free by carrying a piece of paper that said so. If caught without it, he could be sold into slavery. In fact, he was always under threat of being kidnapped and sold. As a free-colored man he was assessed a special tax. Socially and politically, he was under suspicion by whites because they feared his influence over slaves and was despised by slaves because they considered him an ally of whites. He was, to quote the title of one of the best books on the subject of the free person of color in the antebellum South, "a slave without a master."[11]

Restrictions on Chavis's freedom were tightened after every slave revolt or threat of one. By 1861, all southern states and many in the North forbade immigration by free persons of color; and some, including Mississippi and Arkansas, had introduced laws demanding that those already there either leave or sell themselves into slavery. If a free person of color decided to leave wherever he or she was, since so many states prohibited the immigration of free coloreds, some who were light enough simply passed into other states as whites. And some did take the other option, selling themselves into slavery to be allowed to remain near relatives who were slaves. Jordan Chavis was allowed to stay in Mississippi in 1859 only through a specific act of the legislature, prompted by a petition from thirty-three prominent white men in Warren County.

So much for his color. Now, what are we to make of his financial success? How did he get to such a point of affluence that he could afford a generous contribution to the Confederate cause, and what, in light of his color, led him to make it? But first, how did he come to be in Mississippi?

To begin tracing his journey, we can return to his statement in the 1871 claim to the federal government for Civil War reimbursements that he had served in the War of 1812. And indeed, the records show that he served as a private in the Second Regiment West Tennessee Militia under Colonel Leroy Hammons and Captain James Kincaid from September 20, 1814, to March 20, 1815, when he was honorably discharged at Blue Springs, in the Mississippi Territory.[12] Part of General Nathaniel Taylor's Brigade, this regiment was scattered throughout the Creek Territory and the vicinity of Mobile to man the various forts in the region, Forts Jackson, Montgomery, Claiborne, and Pierce. Some of the companies participated in the taking of Pensacola on November 7, 1814.

In reward for this service, in 1851 Chavis successfully petitioned for a warrant for eighty acres of bounty land, which he then sold in 1860 to Oliver Davenport, who located it in Ashley County, Arkansas.[13] (A warrant, like a gift certificate for Walmart, could be used to purchase the designated amount of acreage wherever the government offered public land for sale.)

It was probably during his military service in the Mississippi Territory that young Chavis first laid eyes on the rich soil of the Mississippi Delta, where a few years later he was to seek and find his fortune. Although his company seems to have marched down through what is now Alabama, his discharge at Blue Springs, near Tupelo, Mississippi, suggests that his return home was a walk up the Natchez Trace, the four-hundred-mile path between Nashville, Tennessee, and Natchez, Mississippi, that began as an animal "trace," then was adopted by the Indians and later the Europeans as "the" road through the wilderness. In 1801, Thomas Jefferson put the US Army to work preparing it as a thoroughfare, and by 1809 it was a viable wagon road. On this trip, Private Jordan Chavis would have had ample opportunity to become well acquainted with this formidable, dangerous, treacherous wilderness with soil good enough to offer the promise of a good living to those who could survive taming it.

Mississippi attained statehood in 1817, and in 1829, fifteen years after his march through the territory, Jordan Chavis appears on the tax roll for Claiborne County, Mississippi, a southern county bordered on the west by the Mississippi River, on the north by Warren County, and on the south by Jefferson County.[14] Cotton country. By this time, due to the success of Eli Whitney's cotton gin, the ease with which this invention could be replicated, and the importation of enough slave labor to do the work of raising cotton, that delta soil offered a promise of more than just a good living. It offered wealth to anybody who could obtain title to the land and the labor necessary to clear and work it.

But to backtrack a bit, in March 1813, before his service in the militia would begin in September, Jordan Chavis seems to have had a bit of a windfall that may have provided him with enough capital to start his thinking about a future on the frontier. A man of substance named Aquilla Quick died in Marlboro County, South Carolina, between March 2, 1813, when he made his will, and April 22, 1813, when it was proved. This will bequeathed to one of his daughters, Nancy Chavis, a portion of land from his considerable estate; and in the disposition of the property involved, her husband, Jordan Chavis, signs a number of deeds as grantee.[15] The dates are right for this to have been our Jordan Chavis, but there is no absolute proof in the records. If this is so, Nancy is the only wife ever mentioned in connection with him and so may be the mother of his six children. It is impossible to determine the sum she finally received from the sale of the property, but it is significant that he was able to sign his name for the transfer of deeds while many others had to sign with a mark. Aquilla Quick's ethnicity cannot be determined.

The 1820 US census places Jordan Chavis as head of a household in Murfreesboro, Tennessee, consisting of two free-colored persons, one a male aged between fourteen and twenty-five, the other a male under fourteen. One person is engaged in agriculture. No females are listed and never in any census or land record is there a mention of a wife for Jordan Chavis.[16] However, he had six children, five of whom are listed in census records as having been born in Tennessee between 1818 and 1831.

In 1829, he makes his first appearance in Mississippi public records, in the Claiborne County tax rolls where he is designated "Col'd, Situation: G. B. Congers" (owner of place he lived on). He lists no slaves and is assessed for "1 Free Person of Color, $3.00 state tax, $1.50 county tax, total $4.50."[17]

Like thousands of other immigrants, the Chavises probably moved in wagons from Murfreesboro to Mississippi down the Natchez Trace, by this time a well-traveled road with inns or "stands" spaced a day's journey apart where travelers could spend the night, rest their horses, and purchase necessary items. An 1822 map of Mississippi shows that the length of the Trace from Nashville to Port Gibson was 383 miles. Half the state was still in Choctaw and Chickasaw hands at that time.

In the 1830 census, where his name is misspelled Shavers, he heads a household of nine free-colored persons. His very move into Mississippi was illegal since the passage of a law in 1823, in the aftermath of the 1822 Denmark Vesey "rebellion" in South Carolina, forbidding immigration of free persons of color. And yet there he

is, so described and taxed as such in a legal document. As Charles
Sydnor pointed out in his article "The Free Negro in Mississippi
Before the Civil War," the lines between what was proscribed for
the caste and what was permitted for the individual were blurred.[18]
Otherwise, how can his legal presence be accounted for? Somehow
there was a niche he managed to fit into.

The laws pertaining to the status of free persons of color in
Mississippi were unequivocal. For example, according to Sydnor,
the law assumed that a Negro was a slave unless it could be proved
otherwise, and proof of free status had to be carried at all times in
the form of a certificate obtained from a probate or county court
and renewed every three years. It showed the name, color, stature,
and any distinguishing scars and cost the recipient one dollar until
1831, when the fee rose to three dollars. Any white man employing
a person claiming to be free but unable to produce this certificate
was liable to a fee of ten dollars. And the person of color who could
not produce the document was in danger of being seized by some
unscrupulous white person and held or sold as a slave. Or he might
be jailed, and if unable to establish his freedom within a certain time,
the law required that he be sold at public auction.

He could not go to a different county without running the risk
of being treated as a vagrant, and he could not keep firearms, military weapons, or ammunition without a license, which was voidable
at any time. Free persons of color could sell goods only within
an incorporated town and could not sell groceries or liquor even
there. They could not operate houses of entertainment and they
especially could not work as typesetters in a printing establishment.
The owner of the press who hired one was liable to a penalty of ten
dollars a day for employing such, and for the employee, death was
the penalty for breaking this law. It was feared that a free-colored
person with access to a printing press might be successful in insti-
gating a rebellion against slavery.

Free-colored people could not vote, serve on a jury, or be a witness in a case in which a white person was involved. But they, as well
as slaves, could bear witness in criminal cases against other people

of color or in civil pleas where free coloreds were the parties. In other words, to quote Sydnor, "The civil and political status of the free negro differed from that of his slave brother chiefly in the fact that the slave could not own property while the free negro could."[19]

This was the legal state of affairs for free-colored people in Mississippi when Jordan Chavis landed in Claiborne County. It got progressively worse over the years. In 1831, in the panic following the Nat Turner rebellion in Virginia, a law was passed in Mississippi requiring all free coloreds between the ages of sixteen and fifty to leave the state within ninety days or be sold into slavery for five years. However, those able to prove they had good character and were not "undesirables" could be given a license allowing them to remain. Apparently our man and his family were able to do this; they were truly exceptions that tested the rule.

And yet, the number of free-colored people in Mississippi continued to grow in spite of attempts to keep immigrants like the Chavises out and the passage of new restrictions on the manumission of slaves, the two ways that the numbers of free-colored people could grow besides the third way, the birth of children to free-colored mothers. The year 1840 showed the largest increase in the free-colored population between 1817, the year statehood was acquired, when there were 235 in the entire Mississippi Territory (which was comprised of the present states of both Mississippi and Alabama) and 1860, when there were 773 on the eve of the Civil War. In 1840, the free-colored population reached a peak of 1,366.

In the eyes of whites, something had to be done to hold down the growth in number of a class of people considered dangerous, so in 1840 a new law ordered that if "a free negro entered Mississippi from some other state it was required that he be whipped and ordered to depart within twenty days on pain of being sold as a slave."[20] There was a 31.9 percent drop in the free-colored population of Mississippi between the 1840 and 1850 census reports. Some left the state; a few sold themselves into slavery to be allowed to remain near enslaved relatives.

And yet some did well. Among the successful free persons of

color in Mississippi during this time, perhaps the most notable was a barber in Natchez named William Johnson, whose hard work and astute business sense brought him prosperity and the respect of successful white men. At the time of his death in 1851, he owned three barbershops, a bathhouse, and a plantation. If any free person of color could have felt secure, it would surely have been William Johnson. And yet entries in the diary he kept daily show a man continually looking over his shoulder.

The fine line that successful free men of color had to walk is defined by William L. Andrews in his introduction to *The Diary of William Johnson*, where he shows that the rules limiting Johnson's range of action in his contacts with white people were sometimes obscure and tenuous. On the whole, he was granted something approaching equality in business and financial matters, but he labored under parts of the unwritten code of social restrictions that applied to all persons of color. As Johnson understood only too well, that code contained a provision that prohibited interracial participation, under formal and public conditions, in the rites of eating and drinking, but even this provision was occasionally violated. The barber participated in the raffle of a gold watch at Rowland's Coffee House, and, upon winning half the prize, treated the assembled company to champagne. . . . Two white men who came to see him and his family at his town residence and stayed until after the dinner hour declined to join him in eating but Johnson and his friend McCrary went hunting with white townsmen and ate with them in the field. . . . In other instances, the color line was more sharply drawn. Johnson attended the theatre, but he sat in the Negro balcony. He heard the Reverend John Newland Maffitt, famed Methodist pulpit orator, preach, but he stood outside the church. He was permitted to give financial support to the Jockey Club and make bets with white men, some of whom were prominent professional men, but his horses never ran in scheduled races.[21]

On the occasion of his wife's traveling to New Orleans, William Johnson had to bribe the steamboat's captain to let her have a stateroom, forbidden to blacks by company policy. If he had not been able to do this, she would, perhaps, have endured the conditions the English writer J. S. Buckingham describes in this situation he observed on a boat in Alabama in 1841.

> Among the passengers in the ladies' cabin, were three colored females, going from Mobile to Montgomery, whose position was very remarkable. They were not negresses, but mulattoes . . . , and appeared to be sisters or relatives. They were each dressed much more expensively than either of the white ladies on board—silks, lace, and feathers, with ornaments of jewelry of various kinds being worn by them. They slept on the cabin-floor, as the coloured servants usually do, no berth or bed-place being assigned them . . . [and] they remained sitting in the cabin all day, as if they were on a footing of perfect equality with the white passengers; but when mealtime came, then was seen the difference.
>
> The order in which the meals were taken in the steam-vessel was this: at the first bell the captain and all the white passengers sat down; when these had all finished and left the table, a second bell summoned the pilot, the captain's clerk, all the white men of the engineer's department, the white stewardess, and such white servants or subordinates as might be on board; and when these had finished, the third bell summoned the black steward and all the mulattoes and coloured servants, to take their meal. So equivocal, however, was the position of these coloured ladies, that they could not be placed at either of the tables; they were not high enough in rank to be seated with the whites, and they were too high to be seated with the blacks and mulattoes; so they had to retire to the pantry, where they took their meals standing; and the contrast of their finery in dress and ornament, with the place in which they took their isolated and separate meal, was painfully striking.[22]

Such was the legal morass and social atmosphere in which the Chavis family was able to live, even flourish, until the 1850s.

But if it was the promise of riches that led people to the Old Southwest, what was the quality of life in antebellum Mississippi that encouraged them to pursue it? How did they live there?

To start with, it is certain that the Chavis family lived in a log house. If they were lucky, instead of one room, they had a dogtrot cabin, meaning there would have been two rooms, divided by an open hallway. They probably lived in variations of this cabin on each succeeding place, including the final one in Warren County on the 1,080-acre plantation. As Mississippi frontier farmers prospered, additions were made to the original log house while other buildings, including a kitchen, barn, and slave quarters, were added to form compounds. Many more planters lived in log houses than in mansions throughout the antebellum period, according to contemporary accounts. Solon Robinson, "Pioneer and Agriculturist," who made his living as a journalist for agrarian papers all over the country, visiting Warren and Claiborne Counties in 1845, wrote the following description of a plantation home:

> Now I think I hear some of my eastern fair readers exclaim, "Well now, I do wish he would tell us what sort of a house this Mississippi nabob lives in?—very splendid, I dare say. Oh, I wish I could see it." Well, madam, it is a common double log cabin, with a hall between. "Why, you don't mean to say, that a man with such a farm, and so many negroes, lives in such a house as *that*?"
>
> Oh, yes I do, and very comfortably and nicely he does live too, for he has a wife—ah, a *wife*, madam: not a mere piece of household furniture, such as your boarding school bred farmer's daughter will make—totally unfit for a farmer's wife. "Well, now, do tell me where they all stay in such a house as that?" Why, madam, there is another cabin in the back yard— that is the kitchen—no matter that it is so far off the eating room—it is Mississippi fashion; and there are plenty of negroes to run back and forth; and here is another building—that is the smoke house; and there is another, that is the store room; and there are two or three more, those are the lodging rooms. No matter that they are ten rods from the house—it is the fashion. . . . True, such arrangements would not suit us at the north, but here use and negro labor make the difference.[23]

Most northern writers visiting the South in those days felt compelled to describe the food in derogatory terms. In the winter of 1853–54, Frederick Law Olmsted, visiting Mississippi after a sojourn in Texas, after remarking that the "style of living" enjoyed by Mississippi planters, though superior to that of Texans, was far inferior to that of northern farmers of one quarter of their wealth, had this to say about the food he was served in the homes that he had been at pains to choose as the most comfortable in their neighborhoods:

> I will merely say with regard to diet, that bacon, corn-bread, and coffee invariably appeared at every meal; but, besides this, either at breakfast or supper, a fried fowl, "biscuit" of wheat flour, with butter added—the biscuit invariably made heavy, doughy, and indigestible with shortening (fat) and brought to the table in relays, to be eaten as hot as possible with melting butter. Molasses usually, honey frequently, and, as a rare exception, potatoes and green peas were added to the board. Whiskey was seldom offered me, and only once any other beverage except the abominable preparation which passes for coffee.[24]

Solon Robinson, although giving credit where it was due when he had been served a fine meal with a three-year-old ham and a variety of spring vegetables, including fresh lettuce, to his astonishment available in February, found it necessary to remark facetiously, "It is forbidden by law in Mississippi (the law of indolence,) ever to eat any kind of vegetable matter except 'hog and hominy.'" And again, concerning the food, housing, clothing, and weather, he writes:

> You nor I, Messrs. Editors, never saw a table set in our houses for hireling or even a beggar, with so little variety of eatables as I have often found in public houses and on plantations where negroes were as "plenty as blackberries." Instead of palaces, log cabins that among the yankee race would be considered anything but "comfortable," and the living, whew!
> . . . Whenever you hear any of our northern friends complaining of "hard fare" in a new country, beg of them to follow my footsteps to the south, and if they don't return to their own homes perfectly cured of grumbling, they are certainly incurable. . . . Notwithstanding what I have stated of early

vegetables and warm winter weather here now, and to me
the singular appearance of persons going about barefoot and
without coats, and as I sit writing in a room with windows all
open and the family enjoying the cool shade of the piazza, I
know from what I have seen some frosty mornings, that they
suffer more with the cold than we do in our frozen country.
...An atmosphere at 30 degrees seems colder than it does with
us at zero. . . . And then the heat of summer is undoubtedly
more severe, certainly harder upon the constitution of man
than are the rigors of a northern winter to the inhabitants of
the north.[25]

On the next page, Robinson mentions the prevalence of mosquitoes and flies even in February in Mississippi, which leads us to
consider the problem of disease that these people had to deal with.
Apparently, in households with large families, at any given time
somebody was sick. Kate Stone, in the journal she began keeping
on the family plantation, Brokenburn, some thirty miles west of
Vicksburg, across the river in Louisiana, in 1861, lists, as they happen,
these maladies that repeatedly afflict the members of her family at
one time or another: swamp fever (malaria, typhoid fever, yellow
fever), spasms, whooping cough, measles, diphtheria, consump-
tion, neuralgia, toothache, chills, boils, colds, pneumonia, croup,
and inflamed eyes (probably pinkeye). "Swamp fever" was endemic.
Pneumonia was frequently fatal. There were over a hundred slaves
at Brokenburn and the fear of bringing any disease onto the place
included the fear that it would get into the quarters and spread like
wildfire.[26]

Add to this the life of nature in the yards and surrounding forest. For not only in the woods but in the very yards were several
varieties of poisonous snakes, including copperheads, rattlesnakes,
and water moccasins that would slither into houses as well, there
being no screens for windows and doors. There were bears, wildcats,
panthers, and wolves. Insects were a serious problem; ever present
were mosquitoes, flies, gnats, ticks, and chiggers, a pernicious insect
too small to be seen, but whose bite liquefies the flesh and causes

almost unbearable itching. Poison ivy and poison oak grew every-where. There was also, however, plenty of game.

And we should never forget the ever-present mud on terrain with such deep topsoil and no substrata of rock anywhere near the surface. In winter and during rainy spells, mud in the roads became several feet deep. Sometimes it was buckshot, a coarse-grained, black, gummy clay that sticks like concrete to the feet of humans and horses, and sometimes the mud was quicksand. There were few bridges, and where there was no ferry large enough to take a carriage across a stream, the horses had to swim over and the vehicle had to be dismantled and taken across in a rowboat in pieces and then reassembled.

Such was the nature of life in Mississippi when Jordan Chavis and family were establishing a home there.

CHAPTER 3

Jordan Chavis's Farming Operations in Mississippi, 1830–1860

To answer the question of how Jordan Chavis reached the point of financial security that allowed him to pledge such a generous gift to the Confederacy in June 1861, we need only follow his public records, where we see him climbing rung by rung up the financial ladder. Considering the difficulties presented not only by the frontier, but also by his color, his progress seems fairly remarkable: he first appears in the records in 1829 in Claiborne County living on somebody else's land, with nothing taxable to declare except himself as a free person of color, yet within five years he is able to buy his own farm just across the line in Jefferson County and apparently pay cash for it.

His life was undoubtedly made easier by the circumstance that he and his family apparently did not come to Claiborne County alone. They seem, rather, to have been members of a cluster of highly respected, slave-holding free people of color, some of whom had been born in South Carolina, as Jordan Chavis had, who settled in Claiborne and Jefferson Counties about the same time he did. There is no proof, but logical speculation suggests that members of this group knew each other before migrating to Mississippi and settled there together. It would surely have made a difference that the young pioneer farmer was surrounded by people of his own caste and class rather than solely by white planters and farmers, although, of course, they were in the vicinity as well.

This group of mulatto slaveholders shown to be living near each other in the 1830 US census in Claiborne County included Samuel Martin with one slave; Gloster Simpson, two slaves; Hardy Harris, one slave; and Christopher Holly, three slaves. Also in the community but owning no slaves were Elias Jacobs, Holly's son-in-law, and Jordan Chavis. By the 1850 census, when six of them are shown to be still living one beside another in District 5, their ownership of slaves, and therefore their net worth, had increased considerably. Christopher Holly owned nineteen slaves; Elias Jacobs owned nine; Samuel Martin, eight; Wesley Harris, two; Turner Harris, eighteen; and William T. Livingston owned one slave. By this time Jordan Chavis, owner of ten slaves, was living on his farm across the line in Jefferson County, still near other members of the group, notably the Bolton family, also from South Carolina.

It is a measure of the esteem in which some of these free-colored people were held, particularly the family of Christopher Holly, the most successful and perhaps the most-respected member of the group, that his widow's obituary was printed in the *Port Gibson Reveille* in April 1859:

> The widow of Christopher Holly, a free woman of color was buried yesterday. She died owning a thousand acres of good land and thirty negroes. Her husband lived near town for many years, and was esteemed a gentleman. Holly and his wife were black as any of their slaves, and always conducted themselves well.[1]

But back to the specifics of the Chavises. The whole family is in Mississippi in time for the 1830 US census, where Jordan Chavis is listed as "Jordan Shaver [*sic*]" in Claiborne County, Mississippi, head of a household of nine free-colored persons: one male, aged 24–35; one male, aged 10–23; two males under the age of 10; one female, aged 36–54; one female, aged 10–23; three females under 10.[2] From other evidence we know that some of the ages are right for his children at the time, who were born in Tennessee: Mary Ann was born in 1815; George Washington, in 1818; Jerusha, in 1824; Preston, in 1825; and Hamilton, in 1827. Two little girls under the age of ten on the census list are unaccounted for. A woman the right age to be Jordan's wife is enumerated in this 1830 census, but she never appears again. We know from other sources that Alexander, his last child, was born in 1831 in Mississippi. Perhaps his wife died giving birth to Alexander.

The progress of his rising fortunes can be charted in the tax and census records, which I will summarize here and include in full in an appendix to avoid interrupting the flow of my narrative.[3]

I have noted that Jordan Chavis first appears in the Claiborne County tax rolls in 1829. In 1830 he has nothing to assess except himself, one free person of color, tax due $3.30. By 1833, he has two slaves and is able to sustain this upward track toward prosperity, for in 1836, while still living on Brocus Creek in Claiborne County, he buys 403 acres of land on Clarke's Creek in adjacent Jefferson County for $4,000. In 1840, he still has only two slaves but assesses 460 acres of land. By 1846, he lists seven slaves. It is a terrible mark of those times that the growth of his prosperity is measured by the number of slaves he progressively acquires.

In the 1850 US census he is listed for the first time as "Planter," with real estate valued at $720 in Township 9 East, Jefferson County, Mississippi, and as mulatto, head of household #362 with Mary A. Saucer (daughter); John Saucer, mulatto (son-in-law); "J. Casen [*sic*]," mulatto (daughter), my great-grandmother; and Missouri Casen, mulatto (Jerusha's daughter), my great-aunt. Jordan's age is listed as fifty-three.[4]

In 1853, in Warren County by this time, Chavis is on the tax rolls as a free man of color with eleven slaves, one stallion, eight mares, and thirty-seven bales of cotton. He does seem to be on the path from being a farmer to becoming a planter, as the census taker had already categorized him in 1850.

Then in 1857, he makes a big leap forward, purchasing 1,080 acres of land in Warren County, about ten miles from Vicksburg, for $1,400. At first glance, one might wonder why the price was so modest. Was it because of the depression of 1857 or because most of the land was in woods or because it was seriously gullied? On closer examination, all three possibilities seem to apply.

In 1858, his son Preston buys 107 acres at the Warren County Courthouse door for $345. In the 1860 US agriculture census they are listed next to each other and both seem to be farming

Jordan's large plot because each lists about half the acreage of that 1,080 acres.

Although their combined holdings listed in the 1860 agriculture census do not have cotton production figures, which might have explained exactly how Jordan was able to make his generous contribution to the Confederate cause in 1861, they do indicate the size of their operation and show what they had to lose when the hungry, marauding armies on both sides arrived to take it away from them.

Together they list 1,090 acres, $300 worth of implements, five horses, six mules, sixteen milk cows, ten oxen, seventy other cows, thirty-five hogs, 600 bushels of corn, 100 bushels of peas and beans, 45 bushels of Irish potatoes, 450 bushels of sweet potatoes, and one thousand pounds butter.[5]

The "Slave Schedule" shows Jordan owning ten slaves and ten slave houses.[6] Preston is never credited anywhere with slave ownership.

So that is where Jordan Chavis was in his farming operations in 1860. But where was he in terms of the land he lived on and worked? What did the place look like?

The thought of cotton country inevitably conjures the vision of large, flat fields white with cotton ready to pick. We have seen those fields in movies and in reality in both the Mississippi and Arkansas Deltas. They do exist, but they were not the norm in the terrain that Jordan Chavis dealt with, for there were difficulties with much of the land in Warren County that made farming a more formidable task than one might expect. Apparently, the incredible richness of the soil was a redeeming factor in what would otherwise have seemed a hopeless enterprise. In a column printed in the Albany *Cultivator* in November 1845, Solon Robinson gives the following assessment of the situation in Warren County:

> This county is one of several similar ones along the Mississippi River, and presents a most singular formation. It is called hilly, but I think the word side-hills would convey a more correct idea. It seems to me, from careful examination, to have been a deposit of alluvium two or three hundred feet deep. At the

bottom coarse gravel, then fine, then sand, and then a deposit some ten or twelve feet deep, of fine silex, lime and shells; now a bed of rich marly loam, above which is the fine alumina that was held longest in solution. After this deposit had lain long enough to form a stratum of limestone underneath, it was apparently disturbed by an earthquake, which left the surface in the most uneven condition of any tract of country I have ever seen. I saw many sidehills in cultivation lying at an angle of 45 degrees. . . . There are many farms that do not contain a spot of level land large enough to build a house upon; but the fertility of the soil is so great and so inexhaustible while it remains unwashed away, that it has tempted men to over-come difficulties that never would have been encountered upon poorer land. . . . Though it does not appear to wash away quite so easily as the lighter lands up north, yet I find places here gone past all redemption, and worthless for every purpose except Bermuda-grass pastures, over which nothing could range but sheep and goats. In fact, the whole country looks more suitable for a sheep range than for anything else, and in no part of the United States could wool be raised to better advantage.[7]

It must be remembered that Robinson's ideal is a small, diversified farm worked by its owner and his family with a hired hand or two, prosperous enough to provide a comfortable living. In other words, an operation modeled on a thrifty northern farm, some of which he did find to admire in Warren County. But the kind of life offered by that type of agriculture was not the pull that drew men to the frontier in southern Mississippi. They dreamed of riches, not ample sufficiency, and the only way to fulfill that dream was by owning plantations worked with slaves.

And yet, the list of products raised by Jordan and Preston Chavis in 1860 shows a remarkable degree of diversification. During the war years we will see the addition of sheep to the list of animals, undoubtedly for both meat and wool. As for the lay of the land in hills and gullies, Robinson's description is apt, judging from the way it looked in the autumn of 2013, when I saw it.

CHAPTER 4

The Chavis Children,
1830–1860

The Chavis children are growing up in these years, 1830–1860; and on June 16, 1840, Washington, who would have been about twenty-two at the time, does something extraordinary. He presents the following power of attorney, given him by a neighboring white planter named W. G. Vause, to a justice of the peace, John J. Cross, in Madison, Indiana, to free Synthia, a slave woman, and her two children, Ann and Henry. Although it is never stated in the records, it was understood in the family, according to Washington's great-great-great-great-granddaughter, Kathy Lawrence, that Vause was the father of Synthia's two children.[1] Since no deeds or bills of sale for these people are recorded at the courthouse showing that Washington *bought* them, apparently W. G. Vause simply gave them their freedom. Surely it was an act motivated by conscience.

> Know all men by these presents that I, William G. Vaun [*sic*] of the County of Jefferson and State of Mississippi, have nominated and appointed and by these presents do make and nominate and appoint Washington Chavis, a free man of color, my true and lawfull attorney for me and in my name to convey to either of the State of Illinois, Indiana or Ohio or any other non slaveholding state of this United States my Negro woman slave named Synthia and her two children to wit Ann and Henry, which said Negro woman is about thirty years of age, dark complexion, middle size, with a slight scar in her forehead, and her child named Ann, a bright mulatto girl rather large size, stout made, and about sixteen years of age, and in either of said states where the same may be permitted

by law in my name to emancipate and set free from the bonds
of servitude this same Synthia and her two children Ann and
Henry, my slaves, by any deed or instrument of emancipation
which may be good and effectual for the said purpose and the
same to make seal and deliver and to do all other lawfull acts
and things concerning the premises as fully in every respect as
(if) I myself were present personally.

   Witness my hand and seal at Fayette in said County this
19 day of May A.D. 1840

   Wm G Vaun [*sic*] (seal)[2]

Then, acting in defiance of the law that forbade the return of a
Mississippi slave who had been freed, Washington marries Ann and
returns with her to Mississippi to settle down and raise a family. He
appears for the first time on the 1840 tax rolls for Jefferson County,
where his entry is mostly illegible but lists a tax owed of $1.50.

   In the 1850 census for Copiah, the adjacent county on the east
of Jefferson County, Washington is listed as head of household #777
with his wife, Ann, and children, Calvin, Isaiah, Lewis, and "Parasetta
[*sic*]." Theirs is the only family on the page with a racial designation; they are all designated "M" for mulatto.[3] The "Slave Schedule"
shows his ownership of one black male slave, age twenty-eight.[4]

   In the "Agriculture Schedule," he is listed with 20 acres
improved land and 140 acres unimproved, valued at $300. He owns
farming implements worth $10, one horse, one milk cow, one other
cow, and two hogs, and the value of his stock is $150. His produce
consists of one hundred bushels corn, five four-hundred-pound
bales of ginned cotton, twenty-five pounds of Irish potatoes, and
seventy-five pounds of sweet potatoes; the value of animals slaughtered is $56.[5]

   Washington seems to be on his way. He has a family, land, and a
slave. But within seven years he will feel compelled, because of his
color and free status, to move his family to a safer situation, north
to Illinois.

   As for the other children, Hamilton married Elizabeth Jeffers
on December 5, 1844, in Jefferson County. They had nine chil-

dren. Six were born in Mississippi: Rufus Lafayette, October 27, 1845; Percelar Ann, August 18, 1848; Mary Ann, July 17, 1849; James Putnam, February 8, 1854; T. Monroe, 1855; and Martha Alice, November 10, 1858. Three were born in Arkansas: Cicero, born about 1861; Douglas, about 1863; and Gertrude, about 1866.

Jerusha, my great-grandmother, at age twenty-four married William L. Cason on July 18, 1848, in Jefferson County in her father's house. Not much is known about the groom, but since the marriage was recorded in the "white" book at the courthouse, presumably he was a white man. We know where the wedding took place because in Jerusha's application for a pension due her for William's service in the Mexican War there are the following affidavits affirming the legitimacy of her marriage from two people present at the wedding, two women who were slaves at the time. One, Abigail Bowie, was the cook; the other, Sallie Branch, was a small child.

November 22, 1892

I knew W. L. Cason during his lifetime—I also knew Jerusha S. Chavis who is now Jerusha S. Cason the widow of W. L. Cason—I was present when they were married—I lived with the family of Miss Jerusha—I was a slave at that time, I was the cook and assisted in preparing the wedding feast. I belonged to her father and was living with him when I was set free—I knew when W. L. Cason died, I was not present, but he was reported dead, and his widow came home and lived with her father during his lifetime—I have known Miss Jerusha ever since, and I know that she never married again—She is still a widow.

Redwood, Warren County, Mississippi
(Signed) Abigail X Bowie [her mark]

November 22, 1892

I knew W. L. Cason and Miss Jerusha S. Chavis. I was present when they were married. I was about ten years old but I remember the circumstances quite distinctly. I was a slave, was born on the plantation of Miss Jerusha's father and lived

there until I was set free. I knew her all my life. I remember
when W. L. Cason died, that was more than thirty years ago—I
remember when Miss Jerusha S. Cason came to live with her
father after Mr. Cason died—and I know that she has never
married again. While we don't live near each other now, yet
we hear from her occasionally—We always enquire after our
old folks—

Redwood, Warren County, Mississippi
(Signed) Sallie X Branch [her mark][6]

In her application, Jerusha describes William as about six feet
tall with black hair, a dark complexion, and dark blue eyes. She states
that she no longer has anything with his signature on it because she
lost all her letters from him "during the late war with the states."
Family legend says he fell off a barge and drowned trying to get
mules to Vicksburg during the siege. Jerusha, successful in her claim,
received a pension of eight dollars a month until her death in Ashley
County, Arkansas, in 1907.

William and Jerusha had two children, a daughter named
Missouri, born August 17, 1849, and a son, my grandfather, Albert
Gallatin, born January 12, 1856.

Preston married Laura Ann Jeffers on December 13, 1849, in
Yazoo County, Mississippi. They had no children.

Mary Ann, Jordan's oldest child, married John J. Saucer on
January 22, 1850, in Jefferson County, and they had the following
children, all born in Mississippi: Henry, born about 1853; Willifred,
about 1855; and Andrew, about 1858.

Alexander married Mary Jeffers in about 1853. They had a son,
Jeffers, and a daughter, Florida Clementine, born on May 25, 1854,
in Warren County, Mississippi. Alexander died in a hospital in Little
Rock, Arkansas, in 1862 while serving in the Confederate army.
Preston and Alexander married Jeffers sisters, members of a family
the Chavises probably had known in South Carolina, as well.

In the 1850 census, Preston is listed as head of household #1199 in
Warren County with his wife, Ann, his brother Hamilton, Hamilton's
wife, Eliza, and his younger brother Alexander. The men are des-

ignated "Laborer," which probably means they were working on somebody else's farm, and there is no racial designation on the entire page.[7] In the Warren County tax rolls, #120, J. S. Cason (Jerusha?), is assessed $34.02; #121, P. S. Chavis, $7.57; #122, Hamilton Chavis, $8.84.[8] Perhaps the brothers were working for their sister Jerusha, whose husband was mysteriously elsewhere? Although she and her daughter were living in Jefferson County with Jordan, she and her husband, William L. Cason, may well have owned a farming operation in Warren County.

So, by 1850, the Chavis clan seems positioned to take advantage of what one historian has described as a decade of remarkable prosperity for Mississippi farmers and planters. Crops were excellent and the great mass of the farm population consisted of self-sufficient small operators who were busy acquiring both land and slaves, some rising to the planter class.[9] And although the Chavis family prospers financially during this decade, it becomes clear as we follow their progress that their social and political situation as free people of color becomes more and more precarious as the nation itself moves inevitably toward war over the question of slavery. By 1860, three of Jordan's sons and a daughter have felt compelled to leave Mississippi, and Jordan himself is allowed to remain only on sufferance of the legislature.

CHAPTER 5

Years of Hope/Years of Despair: The Chavis Family in the 1850s

O n the face of it so far, the fortunes of the Chavis family sound like the fulfilled American dream for the nineteenth century. An obviously ambitious, hardworking young man with perhaps a bit of capital goes to the southwestern frontier, works hard, and prospers. Jordan Chavis arrives at exactly the right time for his fortunes to rise with the growth of the cotton kingdom in the Old Southwest, and inch by inch, year by year, his wealth grows. By 1858, the year after buying his 1,080 acres in Warren County, Mississippi, one of his daughters lives in his household and keeps his house and the other lives nearby. Although one son has moved to Illinois, another farms with him and two others are married and live close by, if not in the immediate neighborhood. He has numerous grandchildren.

Considering that Jordan and his family are categorized as "free coloreds" every way they turn, their success sounds almost miraculous. If we had nothing but the legal and financial records charting this individual family's rise to judge by, we might think they had the rosiest of futures and that even with the depredations of the war that we know is about to hit them they might survive and continue to prosper, as many did. But these bare records of what they were able to achieve, in spite of their color, do not begin to tell the whole story of their success, much less of their lives. The records may provide the text of this narrative, but the political and social contexts were even more important. For while it is true that, according to Ira Berlin, "during the 1850's free people of color prospered as never before," it is also true that suspicion and resentment of them throughout the South grew with their success. Berlin describes the situation succinctly in *Slaves without Masters*.

> Their material success, despite all the obstacles whites threw in their path, was apparent in almost every community.... Extravagant signs of free Negro affluence could be seen everywhere: free Negroes employing whites, owning their homes, donning the latest fashions, riding in fancy carriages, flaunting other trappings of success....
> The free Negroes' ability to thread their way through a maze of restrictive obstacles bolstered their confidence and nurtured a new militance. Although they remained a cautious and generally conservative caste, they seemed more willing to challenge white dominance than at any time since the Revolution. To whites, it appeared that the established racial order was under siege.[1]

Their obvious success, as well as tensions surrounding questions about the existence and future of slavery, naturally exacerbated white suspicion of free-colored people; and in every southern state consideration was given to the problem of what to do about it. Radicals thought they should be forced to resettle in Liberia or be enslaved. In the frenzy that engulfed the entire South about what to do with the freemen, it is ironic that Arkansas, the southern state with fewer free persons of color than any other, was the bellwether in the move to solve the problem! This is what the citizens of Arkansas decided to do in the autumn of 1858:

> Under pressure from the governor, the state's leading newspaper, white workingmen and petitions from various public meetings, the legislature hastily ordered Negro freemen to leave the state by 1 January 1860. All free Negroes found in Arkansas after that date would be allowed to choose a master or would be sold into slavery, with the benefits of their sale going to the state school fund. As word of the legislature's decision spread, free Negroes quickly packed their belongings and fled. Some went north to the free states and Canada, others traveled down the Mississippi to Memphis and New Orleans, and a few tried to escape whites altogether by migrating into the Indian territory.[2]

However, before the law was to be applied on January 1, 1860, the legislature backed down and deferred its implementation until 1863. Ironically, while most of the free-colored people of Arkansas were leaving and were practically all gone by 1860, two of the Chavis sons, the oldest daughter, and their families moved to southeast Arkansas in 1859 and declared themselves white! The fire must have looked more promising than the frying pan.

Ominous forces concerning free-colored people were afoot in Mississippi as in the rest of the South in the 1850s, and the Chavis family got caught up in them in spite of their obvious financial success. Christopher Morris describes the situation in Vicksburg and Warren County in the last chapter of *Becoming Southern.*

> 1860 state law forbade slaves from engaging in any sort of trade. The Warren County board of police added a few new restrictions of their own. Slaves found without passes were to receive 39 lashes. All dogs owned by slaves were to be killed. All firearms were to be confiscated. All places of unlawful assembly were to be investigated. Between 1856 and 1860 the state brought 70 cases before the court, charging whites with selling liquor to slaves, trading with slaves, allowing slaves to go at large, allowing slaves to assemble and preach. *At the same time officials cracked down on free blacks, revoking all licenses that granted them permission to reside in the county. Only thirty years earlier Mississippi land speculators advertising for settlers in the Eastern press had made special appeals to free blacks, provided they were of "good character." During the last decade before the Civil War fewer than three dozen free blacks lived in Warren County, nearly all in Vicksburg, and all with special permission from the legislature* [my italics].[3]

The first of the Chavis family to go was Washington, the oldest, who, as we remarked above, in 1840 in Madison County, Indiana, had freed and then married a young slave woman named Ann Vause and moved back to Mississippi with her to farm and raise a family. On January 25, 1855, in Massac County, Illinois, Washington recorded the power of attorney that William G. Vause had given him to free Ann in 1840, establishing the fact of her freedom for the state of Illinois. That same year, he is listed on the Massac County tax rolls alone with his mother-in-law, "Cinthia Voce [*sic*]."

Apparently, his family joined him in 1857, when he bought forty acres of government land in Massac County and recorded new documents proving the freedom of his and Ann's five children so that they could migrate to Illinois.[4] Among the documents recorded was the following new affidavit from "William G. Vaun [*sic*]," which indicates the difficulty free people of color had in simply moving from one state to another.

> Whereas the undersigned William G. Vaun [*sic*] was at one time the owner and possessor of Ann CHAVIS mentioned and described in the forgoing certificate and as such fully entitled in law to her whole issue begotten and born during such ownership and possession and whereas the said undersigned hath heretofore given and granted unto the said Ann CHAVIS and by these presents doth acknowledge and confirm unto her as well as unto Calvin CHAVIS, Isaiah CHAVIS, John Bird CHAVIS, Parasetta CHAVIS and Alexander CHAVIS, the said children of the said Washington CHAVIS and Ann his wife, mentioned and described in the foregoing certificate full unqualified and absolute freedom of person and whereas the said Washington CHAVIS and the said Ann CHAVIS are desirous to remove and emigrate from the said state of Mississippi to the State of Illinois or some other northern or western state and thereto to take with them their said children five in number, as above shown. Know all men by these presents that I the said William G. VAUN [*sic*] do hereby give, grant and impart unto the said Washington CHAVIS, as the said husband of the said Ann CHAVIS, the said Calvin CHAVIS, the said Isaiah CHAVIS, the said John Bird CHAVIS, the said Parasetta CHAVIS and the said Alexander CHAVIS full and absolute leave and permission to travel, emigrate and remove whenever and wheresoever shall be regarded and adjudged proper, meet and suitable by the said Washington CHAVIS and the said Ann CHAVIS. In witness whereof, I William G. Vaun [Vause] of the county of Jefferson and State of Mississippi have hereunto set my hand and seal this seventeenth day of May A.D. 1857.[5]

In the 1860 US census, Washington and his family are listed in a household next to that of "Cinthia Voce [*sic*]," his mother-in-law, in

Massac County, Illinois. Washington is designated a farmer with real estate and personal property valued at $2,500, and Ann is designated a seamstress. Their racial category is "M" for mulatto. In the 1870 census Washington and Ann are listed in the same place with four of their children still at home; three others are listed on their own in the next three households. All the men are listed as "farming."

An immediate question comes to mind that can't be satisfactorily answered, of course, concerning the kind of welcome laid out for free people of color in Illinois in 1855, for in 1848 a new constitution had been adopted by the state that provided, in Article XIV:

> The General Assembly shall at its first session under the amended constitution pass such laws as will effectually prohibit free persons of color from immigrating to and settling in the state, and to effectually prevent the owners of slaves from bringing them into this state, for the purpose of setting them free.

However, in 1853, although the Illinois General Assembly implemented this provision where slaves were concerned, it was relaxed in the case of free people of color. The following statement applied to slaves makes clear the absolute necessity of being able to prove the previous free status of any person of color being brought into the state:

> If any person or persons shall bring, or cause to be brought into this state, any negro or mulatto slave, whether said slave is set free or not, he shall be liable to an indictment, and, upon conviction thereof, be fined for every such negro or mulatto, a sum not less than one hundred dollars, nor more than five hundred dollars, and imprisoned in the county jail not more than one year, and shall stand committed until said fine and costs are paid.[6]

So, when Washington and family arrived, the situation of free-colored people in Illinois seems to have been almost as precarious as it had been in Mississippi. Legally, they were entitled to reside in Illinois, but the attitude implied by the new state constitution is not one of welcome. However, there they all are in the 1860 census, plus two more sons, aged two and three, Jerome and Jordan, all clearly marked "M" for mulatto.[7]

Back in Mississippi, as I have already noted, three more of Jordan Chavis's children, Hamilton, Alexander, and their sister Mary Ann Saucer, were about to exit Mississippi in a different direction, heading a few miles north and west across the river into Arkansas. For if the handwriting about the status of free coloreds in Mississippi was on the wall as early as 1855, when Washington began preparations to leave, it was surely easier to read in 1859.

On December 7, 1859, the following article appeared in the *Weekly Vicksburg Whig*:

A Bill in Relation to Free Negroes

We published a day or two ago a bill in relation to this class of our population. The following bill has been offered as a substitute to the one heretofore published, and it is believed will pass without material modification:

Section 1. Be it enacted by the Legislature of the State of Mississippi, That it shall not be lawful for any free negro or mulatto to reside in this state, without the special license of the Legislature. And any free negro or mulatto found in this state, after the first day of March next, without such license, shall be deemed and held to be in this State without lawful authority, and may be apprehended and sold into slavery for life, as now provided by law.[8]

The remainder of the bill is devoted to defining means of preventing the harboring of free-colored people by whites who pretend they are their slaves and therefore entitled to stay. The next issue of the *Whig* reports that the bill passed by a vote of seventy-five yays and five nays with nineteen members either absent or not voting.[9] The public sentiment leading to the passage of this law in December 1859 would surely have been a matter of concern for some time to free-colored people and would have served as a consideration that led to the decision these people had already made to take their families out of the state.

On June 9, 1857, John J. Saucer, Mary Ann's husband, purchased

160 acres of land in Ashley County, Arkansas, and on December 15, 1859, he bought another 40.[10] On July 18, 1859, Hamilton bought 40 acres in Ashley County, Arkansas, and on April 2, 1860, he purchased another 40. On October 1, 1860, Alexander also bought 80 acres in Ashley County.[11] Hamilton and his family appear in the 1860 census, all designated "W" for white. Apparently, biblical rivers aren't the only streams that can wash one white as snow. For some reason, Alexander and his family and the Saucers are not listed. They may have been en route to Arkansas when the 1860 census taker came round. John Saucer does not appear in the records again; Mary Ann turns up in Ashley County in the 1870 census as head of the household with three children. Jerusha and her son Albert, age fourteen, are listed in the 1870 census in Warren County in Jordan's household, where she is occupied at "Housekeeping" and her daughter Missouri, son-in-law Osborn Jeffrey, and two children are listed next door. They are all categorized "M" for mulatto. Where they all were in 1860 is a mystery. Jerusha, her children, and her grandchildren join the trans-Mississippi Chavis clan, probably in 1875 or 1876. In the 1880 census they too are all white.

As I have already noted, the imagination catches on the hook of practicality at this stunning vision of these three free-colored families moving, in 1859, less than a hundred miles northwestward, as the crow flies, from one slave state to another and becoming white in the process. In other words, they stepped from one state into another in a matter of a few days' travel time while making a quantum leap from one caste to another in what must have been terrifying secrecy. How did they manage it? For one thing, how did they lose so quickly their deferential stance among white people? Because, although they were well-to-do and free, they would still have been expected to behave like colored people all of their lives, up to the point of crossing that river and becoming "white." One wonders how they kept the children silent on the subject of race in their new community. Mary Ann's children would have been six, four, and one. Hamilton's are listed in the 1860 census with ages of fifteen, thirteen, eleven, six, five, and two. Alexander's daughter was six at the time.

People talk. It was up to the census taker to determine racial designation, and even if they were obviously light enough to pass as white, the slightest whisper in the countryside would have influenced his decision. And there were patrols in Arkansas as ready to catch Negroes and sell them into slavery as there were in Mississippi.

And how is it that the stories of this move did not come down to us? Ever. Not a whisper. Mother must have known about it. As I mentioned in the beginning, it is inconceivable to me that there were no stories being told in the family about these times by Albert and Jerusha during my mother's childhood. "Little Grandma," as my mother called Jerusha, lived in Albert's household until her death in 1906 and was directly involved in the raising of the children. According to Mother, it was from her that the girls in the family got their respect for refinement and education. It was Jerusha who engrained in them that most essential ingredient for social standing in the South: how not to be "common." It is one of the many ironies in this story that Mother's white mother was less refined than the so recently "colored" "Little Grandma."

While I understand the reasons behind it, I feel cheated by the silence on the subject of the true nature of their life in Mississippi and the real reason why they left. I strain to recall any hint of these things, and one of the few I have dredged up is the memory of Mother telling about how before the Civil War there were patrols looking for runaway slaves and singing to me the song she said black people sang, "Run, nigger run, the pattyroll git you . . . " I wonder about the context in which she came by that song. By the time Mother was born in 1889, runaway slaves and the patrols chasing them were the stuff of legend. Singing that song is the only time I remember her using the "n" word. Was there, perhaps, a vestigial hint of family fear in the relation of this material to my mother, perhaps by her grandmother? Where else would she have gotten it? Another interesting question is how did Jerusha, as a free-colored member of a slave-owning family, feel about the situation of runaway slaves? How did any of them feel about slavery? And then, I also remember a story told me by a childhood friend while I was in college. My friend, along with Mother, was in a crowded doctor's waiting room one afternoon for long hours, the "white" waiting room, of course. But they could see through a window into the "colored" waiting room that the doctor was taking patients in the order in which they had signed in, not giving preferential treatment to the whites and serving them first. One of the white women finally lost patience and said in a voice that could be heard by all, "Look at that! Can you believe he's taking them ahead of *us*? I think they all ought to be sent back to Africa!" And Mother said, in her quiet voice that could be clearly heard, "How can you say that, Bessie? How would you like to be sent back to Ireland after all these years?" Not the usual public statement by whites in the Delta in 1948.

Regarding the Chavis family's position on the war and, therefore, on slavery, to start with, there is that matter of Jordan Chavis's gift of $500 and a horse to the Confederate cause. Then there is the undeniable fact that exactly one year after Arkansas seceded from the Union, on May 3, 1862, those two newly minted white men, Hamilton and Alexander Chavis, joined the Confederate army in Monticello, Arkansas; and Rufus, Hamilton's oldest son, joined in 1863. Alexander died in service on August 5, 1862, in a hospital in Little Rock, presumably of disease. Hamilton and Rufus returned to Ashley County, Arkansas, after the war and farmed there for the rest of their lives.

By the time Jerusha and young Albert left in the 1870s there were new reasons for African Americans to want to get out of Mississippi, reasons almost as compelling as the ones that prompted the others to leave in the 1850s, but more of that later.

Let us now go back to see what was going on with Jordan Chavis while his children, except for Preston and perhaps Jerusha, were scattering. We left him in 1860, according to the census and tax records, a prosperous farmer in Warren County, living alone and apparently farming, with his son Preston, over a thousand acres. The reason he can still be there is the following petition signed by thirty-three prominent white men asking the legislature to make an exception in his case. The petition is undated but must have been submitted in December 1859 or early in 1860 in response to the bill cited above. Several of the men who signed the petition were neighbors who owned plantations near his place.

To the Hon. The Legislature of the state of Mississippi.

The petition of the undersigned citizens of Warren County respectfully petition your Honorable Body to pass an act authorizing a free colored man named Jordan Chavis to reside in this state. They represent that he is now over 60 years of age & has been a resident of Warren County for many years. They state that he is an honest man, and good citizen and served in the War of 1812. They represent that he is now old and infirm and respectfully submit that it would be cruel and unjust to drive him in his old age from the country he, in his youth, fought to protect.

They, therefore, respectfully ask the passage of an act authorizing him to remain.

(Signed) Herbert W. Hill, Francis M. Lakeman, John E. Patterson, Samuel G. Parks, W. J. Adams, James M. Crump, Thomas P. Bruce, J. S. Ratcliff, J. Snyder, G. B. Sheller, Andrew F. Powell, [illegible], J. H. Goodwin, G. W. Powell, J. A. Dwiggins, James L. Patterson, Tilman Whatly, P. H. Stafford, Silas Smith, Tray Tinsley, Oliver H. P. Wigson, J. C. Harris, G. R. Williams, A. Grant, J. S. Ross, Jas. Crouch, John D. Cato, Wm McIver, Wm. J. White, M. Ford, Thos C. Jones, F. C. Jones, I. B. Hardaway.[12]

No similar petition has been found for Preston, who was, perhaps, allowed to remain because his father needed him in the farming operation. Nor has one been found for Jerusha.

CHAPTER 6

War and Its Aftermath for the Chavis Family, 1861–1873

So, by the end of 1860, the Chavis family is being blown about by that wind made so famous by Margaret Mitchell. The next public notice of Jordan Chavis is the piece in the June 21, 1861, *New York Times* quoted at the beginning of chapter 2. Having answered the questions about his color and the financial status that supported such generosity, we can now turn to the question of why a colored man would be giving financial support to the cause of the Confederacy. The obvious answers that come to mind are simple: First, he wanted to save his neck, and, second, he wanted to save his property, including slaves, which would only be done by a victorious Confederacy.

But he is caught in this dilemma: If the Confederacy wins, he will be able to keep his property but he will also still be a social outcast with no hope, according to the *Dred Scott v. Sanford* decision of the US Supreme Court, delivered on March 6, 1857, of ever being considered a citizen of the United States. This decision is explicit that persons of African descent cannot be, nor were ever intended to be, citizens under the US Constitution.

If the Union wins, and he may secretly hope it does, as he later swears, he will lose his slaves, his biggest investment and his essential labor force. However, he may hope to be a citizen some day with all the legal rights, privileges, and social standing that might accompany full citizenship. The catch, of course, is that if some of his neighbors suspect, in 1861, that he is a Union man, he most likely will not live to enjoy those rights. So whatever he believes in his heart of hearts, best hedge his bets and publicly support the Confederacy with all the means at his disposal. Five hundred dollars and a horse make a good first statement.

On the other hand, things were even more complicated than this, according to personal statements Jordan Chavis makes, under oath, in 1871. For on March 3, 1871, the US Congress approved an act allowing citizens who could prove their loyalty to the Union during the war to claim reimbursement for property taken from them for use by Union forces. It did not allow for reparations to be paid for destroyed property but for items taken to sustain Union troops. On September 19, 1871, Jordan and Preston Chavis filed separate claims for payments they felt due them, because of their loyalty, for their stock and feed taken by Union foraging parties in June 1863, shortly before the fall of Vicksburg.

Their testimony is interesting for several reasons, not least because it stirs the muddy waters of their real intentions and feelings. Jordan Chavis is, after all, a colored man now attesting his loyalty to the Union, albeit a colored man who had owned slaves and stood to gain financially, but not personally, by a Confederate victory. But he is also a colored man who believes he suffered grievously at the hands of the Union army sent there to free him from the bonds of his color. At no point in the course of his suit against the government and the government's countersuit against his claim is his contribution to the Confederacy of $500 and the horse ever mentioned. But the hoped-for favorable resolution of his claim, which remains in limbo until eighteen years after his death, is finally caught on the hook of a different tie with the Confederacy.

This testimony is also interesting as witness to the depredations of war. This is the way it happened, Jordan tells us, and provides two witnesses who also saw his property taken. They are two of his former slaves, Thadeus Branch and Nero Bowie. Here is the testimony Jordan Chavis gave, first in a personal statement and then in answer to questions in cross examination:

> I am seventy eight years of age—nearly 79—reside near Haynes Bluff, Warren County Miss. In the spring & summer of 1863 U.S. soldiers took from me for the use of the U. S. Army,

eight horses worth $800, eighty head of cattle worth $800, eight hundred bushels of corn worth $800, thirty-seven sheep worth $111, forty-five hogs worth $135 & one wagon worth $100. Said property belonged to me. I never have been paid therefor. I have always been loyal to the U. S. I was born free & have always been free. I served as a soldier in the U. S. Army in the war of 1812 in the 2nd regiment west Tennessee. At the commencement of the rebellion I owned a plantation of over a thousand acres of land near Haynes Bluff—well fenced & stocked. My claim above stated does not include near all the property taken by U. S. soldiers to my information and belief.[1]

In the section of the claim establishing his loyalty to the Union, Chavis states that in June of 1863, shortly before the fall of Vicksburg, when the events in his claim took place, his plantation lay between the lines of the two armies, and that he remained there until the winter of 1864, when he moved to Yazoo County, near Sartartia, where he lived for about two years. In answer to questions about his loyalty, he swears that he never supported the Confederate cause in any way. He says he was never arrested by the Confederates but was so by Federal troops when he crossed their line in an attempt to recover goods they had taken from him and was kept three days in prison by them. His negative answers to some specific questions about aid to the Rebels are, of course, downright lies, and one of them will be caught in the fine-tooth comb applied by federal investigators on down the line. But in this initial go-round the question of his loyalty is answered satisfactorily. Here is his answer to the question of where his sympathies lay at the beginning of the rebellion:

> I sympathized with the Union cause. I said the rebels were doing wrong and acting foolish—said all I dared to say. I wanted the Union to be maintained—thought it the best government ever established. I never wanted it destroyed. I talked that way all the time to those whom I knew to be Union men. It would not do to talk it to rebels.

In cross-examination about the actual seizure of the property, Chavis gave this testimony:

I was present when part of the things were taken. I saw them take three horses, five or six cattle, saw them take five sheep and running after others, saw them take the wagon, saw them take five hogs. Saw them take the corn. . . . It was taken at different times. . . . There was an officer there at the taking of the corn & horses. Don't know name or rank. . . . A squad of soldiers with 14 wagons came at one time & took probably 400 bushels of corn, they came a good many times afterward & took the rest. A company of cavalry took the three horses— said they were the kind they wanted. The hogs, cattle and sheep were killed on the place, a few at a time . . . & the meat jacked off by the soldiers. . . . It was taken off in the direction of the Union Camp at Blake's place about 3 miles distant. . . . I did not follow. Their line run through my place & they would not let me pass through.

The corn was dry in the crib. The horses were all good animals. I had been offered $200 a piece for some of them. The cattle were mostly milch cows, ten dollars a head is a very low estimate. The hogs were good average hogs. I have put in everything at a very low estimate. I never measured the corn but estimate it from size of crib—believe there was a thousand bushels. Know there were 800—it was all taken. I had 15 horses & they were all taken but three. I claim pay for but eight to be surely within bounds. I had 125 head of cattle when the army came; when it left, I found four. I saw soldiers frequently taking off the animals. Can't tell the exact number.

In answer to the question of whether he had ever contributed anything in aid of the US government or in aid of the Union army or cause, he replied, "I have given my acquaintances & friends in the Union Army money for their assistance a good many times." In answer to the question of whether he had any near relatives in either the Union or Confederate armies, he gave this reply, "I had one son, Alexander Chavis, in the Union Army. I contributed nothing to his equipment. He was in Arkansas, didn't come down here." This was, of course, another blatant lie, both Hamilton and Alexander having joined the Confederate army in 1862.

And of course Chavis answered "No" to the question of

whether he had ever owned any Confederate bonds or had in any way contributed to support the credit of the Confederate states during the late rebellion.

The witnesses, Thadeus Branch and Nero Bowie, both former slaves of his, testify to the seizure of property, their statements differing from Chavis's only in the exact number of animals, the amount of corn taken, and their estimates of the value of the goods taken. As for Chavis's loyalty to the Union, Thadeus Branch had this to say, "I was intimate with claimant during the war and saw him about three times a week. We conversed often about the war and he said he did not care much about the war[;] he was always a free man and would like to see all slaves free."

According to the court records, the case was dismissed by the US Court of Claims "about" December 6, 1873, because of doubts about Jordan Chavis's loyalty to the Union. The government's plea was that the testimony of the witnesses showed no *acts* of loyalty; *sentiments* of loyalty were not sufficient.[2]

Jordan Chavis died ten days later, on December 16, 1873. The following record appears in the Fisher Funeral Home accounts for December 16, 1873: "Chavis, Jourdan, W. Chavis on Acct. Of Jourdan Chavis, Deceased, Dr. To one Black Walnut Coffin & Box, ½ Sattin Lined Silver Plated Handles—$50.00."[3] His place of burial is unknown but is thought to have been on his own land.

Preston's claim for reimbursement was filed in 1871 at the same time as his father's and also denied because of doubts about his loyalty to the Union during the war.

Here is his personal statement:

> I live near Mill Dale, Warren County. In the spring of 1863 U. S. soldiers took from me for the use of the U. S. Army six horses worth $660, forty two head of cattle worth $840, one wagon worth $100, one hundred bushels of corn worth $100 & ten hogs worth $50 . . . counting altogether to $1750, said property belonged to me in my own right. I have always been a free man. I have never been paid for said property or any part thereof. The reason I did not see the whole of my property taken was because I went to the Headquarters of Generals

McCarter and Frank P. Blair to obtain a protection paper for
my property and when I returned all my property was gone
and though I did not see them in the act of taking it I saw
some of it in their possession afterwards.[4]

Probably because the claim is restricted to reimbursement for
property taken to be used by the army and not for reparations for
property destroyed by the troops, he does not also relate that while
he was gone to the Union camp to beg for the protection paper,
the soldiers burned his house. According to an eye witness quoted
in the 1886 reopened claim, the soldiers said they did not believe
it belonged to Preston Chavis but thought he was taking care of it
for absent white people, so they burned it down!

In answer to the question of whether he had had any relatives
in the Confederate army, Preston replied, "Not as I know of."

Here is the final question in his cross-examination, "Interrogatory
33": "At the beginning of the rebellion, did you sympathize with
the Union cause, or with the rebellion? What were your feelings
and what your language on the subject. On which side did you
exert your influence and cast your vote? What did you do, and
how did you vote on ratifying the ordinance of secession? After the
ordinance of secession was adopted in your state, did you adhere to
the Union cause, or did you 'go with the State?'"

And Preston's answer was this: "I exerted my influence on neither side. I was obliged to be neutral—I was not allowed a vote. My
feelings were with the Union Cause but I was *obliged* to go with
the state."

Preston's witnesses were three white Confederate veterans who
swore to his possession of the property he claims was taken, to
his feelings as a Union man, and also to his good standing in the
community.

I am 41 years old reside in Warren County near Haines
[*sic*] Bluff, I am a farmer, I have known the claimant about
12 years. I have always known him to be a strictly honest &
upright man. I always looked upon him as a Union man[;]
he was not allowed to express his opinion openly. I was in

the Confederate Army but knew the claimant to be a good citizen. I know that he had about 5 or 6 horses and cattle & corn but what quantity I could not say. I saw claimant just after the fall of Vicksburg but he had none of his property left. I did not see them taken. I only know what he had as I lived only about 3½ miles from him, I can honestly say that he was a good honest Union Citizen and this is about all I could state as I did not see the taking.

Signed: John E. Patterson

I am 44 years old. I live in Warren County 7 miles from Vicksburg. My occupation is Agent for Plantations. I have known the claimant about 18 years. I was not intimate with him during the war. I was in the Confederate Army and he was at home. Except up to September 1862 when I went into the army. The claimant always said that the U. S. Government was good enough for him as it was—he was a free colored man. I know that Claimant had 6 or 7 head of horses worth about $125 per head—he had about 40 head of cattle grown & partially grown worth 15 to $20 per head—he had about 100 bushels of corn in the ear and in the shock already in the crib and ripe—he had some hogs but I could not say the number. I never saw these things taken. I only know that he had them and he did not have his house even when I saw him again which was about June 1865.

Signed: Samuel G. Parks

I knew him intimately during the war up to December 1863 when I moved out from there to Yazoo co and in 1864 I went into the army—the Confederate Army—I knew that claimant had about 6 or 7 horses, worth about 130 to $140 per head, about 40 head of cattle about 15 to $20 per head, and about 300 to 400 bushels of corn. I was at Haines Bluff at Claimants house about 3 o'clock in the evening when the soldiers of the U. S. Army were at Sniders bluff and I then went home to attend to my own affairs. I saw him about 2 months after the U. S. troops had passed through and he had nothing

left not even a board to put his head under. I have always
known him to be a good law abiding citizen, he was a free
colored man and he has said he was a union man. This is all I
know about his case that he was bitterly opposed to the war.
He was one of the best neighbors in the settlement (although
a colored man) every man respected him and he was the same
to me as any other neighbor. I was myself opposed to the war
but when all my property was taken I went in the army and
did my duty. These facts are all that I know about his property
as I did not see it taken.

Signed: Joseph W. Parks.

Joseph Parks's ambivalence about the Confederate cause, which
he finally served, is testimony to the mixed feelings of many of the
residents of Warren County toward the war. Incidentally, it was he
who sold Jordan Chavis his 1,080 acres of land in 1857.

Preston Chavis's claim was disallowed about December 9, 1872,
on the ground that the commissioners were not convinced of his
loyalty during the war of the rebellion.[5] It too was taken on by his
nephew Alexander in 1886 and pursued until 1892.

From the testimony in both these claims filed in 1871 we know
something about how Jordan and Preston spent the war years. They
hung on at Haynes Bluff until 1864 and then went a few miles
away to Yazoo County, where they remained until 1866. There were
several good reasons for them to leave in 1864. First of all, the area
where they lived was constantly harassed by Confederate gueril-
las; but worst of all, perhaps, was the massive appearance of army
worms that devastated the cotton crop. Cotton production in the
Vicksburg district that year was reduced from forty thousand to
eight thousand bales![6]

Then Jordan and Preston Chavis returned to Warren County
in 1866 and took up where they had left off. For by the spring of
1867, Jordan was home again and back in business farming, apparently successfully, since on March 4, 1867, he mortgaged his 1,080
acres to Julius Hornstal for $1,200, payable November 1, 1867. This
is obviously furnish money to make his crop, and he was able to pay
the debt in full on December 12, 1867.[7]

But on September 1, 1868, Jordan sells his 1,080 acres to his daughter Jerusha for $1,200 in cash.[8] One wonders if this transfer of ownership took place as a hedge against the family's losing the land, in case he had to declare bankruptcy, as so many farmers were doing. (This is precisely the action taken in 1868 by my paternal great-great-grandfather Uriah Jones, who transferred ownership of his land to my grandfather Joseph to keep it in the family after his personal bankruptcy.) Or, had Jordan borrowed "furnish money" from Jerusha and had to pay it back with title to his land? On October 21, that same year, for another $350 in cash he sells her "one black mare mule, one brown mare mule and one bay mare mule, also my interest in and to the crop of corn, cotton, potatoes, etc., raised by me on the plantation where I am residing near Ball Ground in Warren County, Miss. And known as the Hardaway Place."[9] Another question is where Jerusha could have found the money to pay him with, if indeed money did really change hands in the transaction. Another ominous sign is that Preston's taxes of $52 are listed as delinquent for 1868.[10]

On January 1, 1870, we can account for Jordan and his children this way: Preston and his wife as well as Jerusha and her family are still in Mississippi with him; Washington and his family are in Illinois; Hamilton and Alexander had joined the Confederate army in 1862 and Alexander died in service after a few months. Hamilton returned to Ashley County, Arkansas, at the end of the war and is still there with his family. Mary Ann, unaccounted for throughout the 1860s, appears in the 1870 census in Ashley County as "Mary Suser [sic]," head of household, with her three children. Her husband, John Saucer, is nowhere to be found in the records, so is presumably dead.

Although, on one hand, the Civil War and its outcome left Jordan Chavis balanced on a tightrope over financial ruin, on the other, it freed him along with the slaves. With the ratification of the Fourteenth Amendment to the US Constitution in July 1868, he and his kin became citizens of the United States, wherever they were, even in Mississippi! One can only imagine the feelings this turn of events must have brought to the family. Although they would still be

categorized "M" on census records and looked upon as "colored,"
the men, at least, should soon be able to vote and all could now bear
witness against whites in courts of law. They could even aspire to
public office. If these things were possible in the place of their birth,
maybe the exiled sons could come home. And apparently the surviving sons who had felt forced to leave in the 1850s begin to think
of returning to Mississippi in 1870.

The Chavis family seems to be poised on the threshold of a new
life, standing on one of those peaks where the greatest promise of
America, the promise of equality for all, looks possible. Of course,
the snake lurking in this new Garden of Eden is the problem that
their dream of such a future is the southern white man's nightmare.
Everything the family stands to benefit from in Reconstruction
is considered a threat to southern white people, and the Chavises
stand to lose everything if the federal government reneges on its
promise of support. But since they are unaware in 1870 of what is
coming, the exiles make plans to come "home." Remember, Jordan
is still alive, Preston and his wife and Jerusha and her children are
with him, and as long as the land remains in the family there is still
a spot in Warren County that they can identify as "home."

Perhaps this is why Hamilton buys 200 acres of land in Warren
County on May 2, 1870. He pays $20 down and is to pay $890 on
January 1, 1871, and $890 on January 1, 1872. The deed is delivered
to Jordan Chavis on July 14, 1870.[11] Nothing more is on record
about this land and Hamilton never moved back to Mississippi, but
at least for a time he seems to have intended to.

And Washington actually does return to Mississippi to live.
According to the US census, on July 2, 1870, he is still in Massac
County, Illinois, surrounded by family, listed as a farmer with real
estate worth $1,200 and a personal estate valued at $300. Some of
his children are still in his house and three sons are married and
head adjacent households.[12] But on December 18, 1871, he leases
30 acres from Margaret Roach on the Ball Ground Plantation in
Warren County to farm the next year. This land is, if not adjacent
to his father's place, very close to it. Rent was "forty pounds of

ginned cotton per acre of the first picking baled & delivered to Haynes Landing." He gives her a lien on his corn and cotton crop as security.[13]

Financially, the 1870s seem to begin well enough for Jordan Chavis. Not only is the family still in business, but on April 2, 1870, he buys another 240 acres on Ball Ground Creek for $960 ($200 down, $760 to be paid when clear title is provided).[14]

In the 1870 population census, taken on June 30, although Jerusha now owns the original property, Jordan is listed as head of household #128 that includes Jerusha, age forty-one; her son Albert, age fourteen; her daughter Missouri, age twenty-one; Missouri's husband, Osburn Jeffrey, age twenty-eight; and their children, William W., age three, and James W., age one. All are categorized "M" for mulatto.[15] Preston is listed as head of household #124. Households #122 and #123 are headed by Thad Branch and Sally Branch, respectively, known from their testimony in claims made by Jordan and Jerusha to the federal government to have been former slaves of Jordan Chavis.

And in the 1870 agriculture census, where his name is misspelled "Chaffer," Jordan is listed with 1,180 improved acres and 100 woodland acres with the value of $3,000, as though they are still his; implements worth $170; one horse, one mule, five milk cows, two oxen, six other cattle, thirteen sheep, and six hogs with the value of $627; and four hundred bushels of corn.[16]

Osburn Jeffrey lists 10 improved acres valued at $60; implements worth $18; and one horse, one mule, nine cows, eight sheep, and one hog with the value of $280.

Preston, whose name is also misspelled "Chaffer," lists 20 improved and 100 woodland acres valued at $600; implements worth $140; three horses, one mule, one milk cow, eleven other cows, ten sheep, and twelve hogs with the value of $790; and one hundred bushels of corn.

Presumably the families farmed together, sharing work animals, implements, and labor. But things are not going as well as they seem. In the 1871 *List of Insolvent and Delinquent Taxes,* Jordan is shown owing $250; and Washington, $132.[17]

It is at this point that Jordan and Preston decide to press for reimbursement for property taken by the Union troops during the war and file the claim we have noted above. Indeed, the settlement of those claims in their favor would have solved their immediate problems and perhaps put the family on solid financial ground once more. However, this not being the case, when Jordan died intestate on December 16, 1873, this failed claim was all in the world he had left. And it must have been festering in the family's "might have been" list of "what if" fantasies for years until Washington's son, Alexander, took it up and sued the government again in 1886.

FIGURE 4. Washington Chavis,
Jordan Chavis's son, in 1874.
*Courtesy Library of Congress
Prints and Photographs Division.*

FIGURE 5. Jerusha Chavis Cason, Jordan Chavis's daughter, and her son Albert
Gallatin Cason ca. 1862. *Courtesy Janice Campbell George.*

FIGURE 6. Preston and Hamilton Chavis, Jordan Chavis's sons? Positive identification is impossible. Tintype was passed down through Hamilton's family. *Courtesy of Jean Chavis and Donna Preston.*

FIGURE 7. Parzeda Chavis Harrison, Washington Chavis's daughter, holding baby.
Others in the photograph are members of her daughter-in-law Irene Marshall's
family. *Courtesy Kathy Lawrence.*

FIGURE 8. Captain Jordan
Chavis, Washington Chavis's
son. *Courtesy Manuscripts,
Archives, and Rare Books
Division, Schomburg Center
for Research in Black Culture,
New York Public Library,
Astor, Lenox, and Tilden
Foundations.*

FIGURE 9. Albert Gallatin
Cason, Jerusha Chavis
Cason's son. *Author's
collection.*

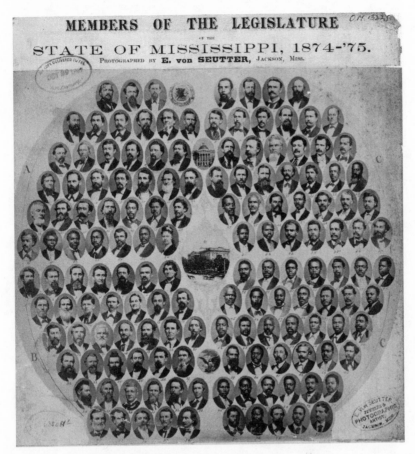

FIGURE 10. Mississippi legislature, 1874–1875. *Courtesy Library of Congress Prints and Photographs Division.*

Reconstruction and Ruin,
1873–1882

After Jordan Chavis's death on December 16, 1873, Washington did not get around to settling his father's estate right away because at the time he had a lot more on his mind than the family's legal affairs. He had taken up politics and, exercising his new rights under the Fourteenth and Fifteenth Amendments, had run for office; and on November 5, 1873, he was elected a representative for Warren County in the Mississippi legislature on the Republican ticket for the 1874–1875 term. Unfortunately, his entry into politics coincided with the exact moment in history when the whites in the South realized that there was enough national sympathy with their cause to allow them to put a stop to blacks voting. Which they proceeded to do with violence and intimidation almost equaling the force they had used to keep the slaves in line before emancipation. Vicksburg was the epicenter of the explosion.

Because of a political split between the "home Republicans" and the deeply resented "carpetbag Republicans" in Mississippi, enough white Republicans switched their votes to the Democratic ticket in the August 1873 state and county elections to allow black Republican voters, the majority, to nominate and sweep their candidates into office in impressive numbers. Black membership in the legislature increased from 42 in 1871 to 60 in 1874, nowhere near a majority in the 150-member body but, in the eyes of whites, certainly a growing threat. Furthermore, the Warren County Courthouse was controlled by a political machine dominated by African Americans.[1] Of course this was a matter of deep concern for white people who feared a take-over of everything by the black majority, a situation they considered intolerable. The Republican machine running Warren County was considered by whites to be totally corrupt, with office-holders skimming money acquired by excessive taxation for personal use. It did not help that the purpose claimed for the high tax rate was the establishment of schools for black children.

Consequently, for the black citizens of Mississippi, as well as the rest of the South, what had looked like the beginning of the best of times shortly turned into a situation almost as bad as slavery, the worst of times. The start of the "Vicksburg Troubles" in the summer of 1874 was the beginning of a steady march by whites toward destroying the black vote, which culminated in the adoption of the "Mississippi Plan," as outlined in 1875 by a proponent, W. Calvin Wells, secretary of the Hinds County Democratic Campaign Committee. Here, in summary, is his list of the policies to be followed in implementing it: (1) organize a solidly Democratic front; (2) intimidate Negroes if persuasion fails; (3) stuff the ballot box with Democratic tickets; (4) destroy Republican tickets; (5) substitute Democratic for Republican tickets for illiterate Negroes; (6) and if these plans do not work, then count out the Republicans and count the Democrats in.[2]

The treatment of black people in Mississippi in the summer of 1874 invites comparison with Eastern European pogroms and German harassment of Jews during the Third Reich, minus concentration camps. One incident of violence and intimidation followed another, but the one most germane to our story was the arrest of the sheriff and the take-over of the Warren County Courthouse in December of that year, for Washington's son Calvin Chavis was present at one of the pivotal moments of the "troubles." He was deputy sheriff to Peter Crosby, a black Union army veteran who had been elected sheriff in 1872 and whose removal from office on December 2, 1874, by a mob of some five hundred armed white men under the guise of the Taxpayers' League was the match struck to the political tinder already laid for the fire. Calvin Chavis was in the sheriff's office when the white men took over the courthouse and seized Peter Crosby.

The event is described by Nicholas Lemann in *Redemption: The*

Last Battle of the Civil War. Put very simply, this is what happened. The specific charge against Crosby was that since his bondsmen did not have the assets they had claimed to have as surety for the bonds they signed to underwrite his election, he was not legally sheriff of Warren County. So they felt entitled to invade the courthouse, arrest him in his office, and demand his resignation. To save his life, Crosby agreed to resign, under protest, and in exchange was allowed to leave the building. He went to Jackson that night and reported the incident to the carpetbag Republican governor, Adelbert Ames, who advised him to return to Vicksburg, raise a *posse comitatus*, or temporary militia, and restore the courthouse to its elected officials. Ames then issued a proclamation calling for the white men of Warren County holding the courthouse to disperse. In Vicksburg, Crosby also issued a circular, ending with this peroration:

> Citizens, shall we submit to violent and lawless infringements on our rights? No; let us with united strength oppose this common enemy, who, by all the subterfuges known to political tricksters, and the audacious mendacity of heartless barbarians, are trying to ruin the prospects and tarnish the reputation of every republican, colored or white, who aspires to fill any office of prominence, and who are daily defying the constituted powers of the law and insulting those charged with its administration.[3]

On Sunday, December 6, black ministers all over Warren County read this proclamation to their congregations and urged their participation in Crosby's effort. By Sunday afternoon a black *posse comitatus* was forming in the countryside outside Vicksburg. On Monday morning this militia of black men, some 400 and heavily armed, according to whites, though fewer and less well armed, according to blacks, approached Vicksburg. Warned by a sentinel, a group of some 150 white men met them and a bloody fight followed. The number killed varies with different accounts, but the term "slaughter" was frequently used to describe the murder of blacks. On that afternoon, there were two other encounters on the roads leading into Vicksburg; and afterward, on through 1875, groups of white men roamed the countryside searching for arms and seeking vengeance by killing black men.[4] According to Eric Foner, as many as 300 black men may have been murdered, not by men hiding under hoods, as members of the Ku Klux Klan had operated, but undisguised, in broad daylight.[5]

The "Vicksburg Troubles" caught the attention of the nation and a congressional investigation was promptly called for on December 14, 1874:

> Resolved, That a committee of five be appointed by the Speaker to proceed to Vicksburgh, in the State of Mississippi, and investigate and report all the facts relative to the recent troubles in that state, and especially in Warren County; committee to have power to send for persons and papers, and administer oaths, and have leave to report at any time. The Speaker appointed as said committee: Mr. Omar D. Conger, of Michigan: Mr. Stephen A. Hurlburt, of Illinois; Mr. Charles G. Williams, of Wisconsin; Mr. R. Milton Speer, of Pennsylvania; Mr. William J. O'Brien, of Maryland.[6]

Calvin Chavis's presence in Crosby's office when the arrest took place made him a key witness for the committee. They questioned him not only about the specifics of Crosby's arrest that day and the accusations about the legitimacy of his bonds but about the general atmosphere of intimidation of blacks to prevent their voting in the August city election, when a white militia had taken charge of Vicksburg and patrolled the streets. His testimony corroborated suspicions members of the committee already had that this harassment had caused a number of black people to leave. As for Peter Crosby's arrest, according to Calvin Chavis, it went this way: At first a committee of ten white men came to the office and requested that the sheriff go with them. He replied by inviting them to come into his office instead, which they did. They told him they had been sent to request his resignation. When he asked for the reason, they said they were not instructed to answer that, merely to get his resignation. He replied, saying he did not know of any reason why he should resign but that he would consult his attorney. They left. In about an hour, they returned in force. Here is a transcript of some of Calvin's testimony before the committee:

Q. How many came in your room there in the office?

A. I don't know; a good many.

Q. Did they fill it pretty well?

A. Yes sir, they filled it pretty full. . . .

Q. What was it they told him?

A. That they wanted him to resign.

Q. What did he say?

A. He did not say much of anything, and they told him he had to resign. Somebody made the remark that he could not be sheriff more than one hour longer. I don't know who that were; but they fixed up a resignation. Mr. Marshall wrote it, I think. . . .

Q. Did he say anything when he signed it?

A. I understood him to say that he did it under protest.

Q. What was said to that by any of them?

A. They did not say anything; they were all laughing and hallooing and shouting; they seemed to be rejoicing.

Q. It was not entirely quiet there then, was it?

A. Well, it was right blustery. . . .

Q. I wish you would give me an idea about how many men there were crammed into that room.

A. I should suppose there was twenty in the office, maybe more; people were crowded all around there; it was impossible to get into the door. . . . I was standing on a stool in there.

Q. Did Crosby ask them for any time?

A. He wanted to go out; they told him that he could not go, some of them.

Q. Did they tell him that he could not go out until he signed that resignation?

A. Yes, sir. . . .

Q. The court-house was pretty full of people?

A. Yes, sir; a big crowd.

Q. How many do you think there were in the whole crowd?

A. I don't know; two or three hundred, I suppose.[7]

Calvin's testimony is interesting not only for the information he gives as an eyewitness to the arrest of Peter Crosby and the chilling effect recent events had had on the black population but also for its indication that his personal situation between a rock and a hard place was as perilous, in its way, as his grandfather Jordan's situation had been when Mississippi seceded from the Union. His life is on the line; one mistake, and his future will be seriously in doubt. So he is cagey in his answers and absolutely refuses, on occasion, to name names. For example:

Q. Was there violence offered to Judge Brown?

A. Not that I know of.

Q. Did you hear of any violence to Judge Brown?

A. I did not hear of any at all.

Q. Did you hear of any threats?

A. I heard threats.

Q. When and from whom?

A. I shall not tell.

Q. You say you heard threats against Judge Brown?

A. Yes, sir.

Q. You decline to say from whom?

A. Yes, sir.

Q. The oath you have taken was to tell the whole truth; you should have said this before you were sworn; now do you decline to tell the whole truth?

A. I will tell the whole truth but not that part of it.

Q. Why did you take such an oath, then?

A. What I told you will be just like the gentleman said; if I tell you a falsehood it will be unintentional.

Q.You claim under the oath to state what you please and withhold what you please?

A. I don't propose to testify in reference to that. I don't propose to have anything to do with it.[8]

Later, the chairman of the committee comes back to the question of why Calvin is reluctant to give names:

Q.Will you state to me why you decline to answer to particular persons here?

A. Well, I expect to live here in this country. I want to live here friendly to everybody, and I do not want people to have hard feeling with me, for that is something I can let alone; and I prefer not to say anything about it.

Q. Do you decline to answer the question because of the consequences upon you?

A. Yes, sir.

Q. Of consequences that you think might be injurious to you?

A. Might be; I don't know.

Q Is that the view with which you decline to answer this question?

A. Yes, sir.

Q. Do you decline to answer the question from motives of personal injury?

A. I don't know as I would be personally injured.

Q.You think it might affect your prospects as a politician in this country?

A. I don't know; I don't consider myself a politician. I think I could get a living without it.

Q. In which view do you decline—from an apprehension of personal violence, or from an apprehension of injury to your business by any persons?

A. I never looked at it in this way. I am friendly to the parties that I heard say these things, and they are as much

friends to me as Judge Brown is. I do not feel like doing
or saying anything that would injure the feelings between
me and those parties.

Q. You do not want to go away from here?

A. I want to live here friendly with everybody.[9]

Perhaps to determine that Calvin was familiar enough with
the local situation to make judgments about the relations between
blacks and whites in Warren County, he was asked for some personal
information:

Q. How long have you lived in this country?

A. I was born and raised in this country but went from here
when the war broke out, and went to Illinois and lived
there until 1871.

Q. Has your father's family been living here some time?

A. Yes, sir.

Q. I believe your family never was in slavery?

A. Yes, sir.

Q. You belong to the class known as the free colored people
here, before the war?

A. Yes, sir.

Q. Is your father this old gentleman who is representative of
the legislature from this county?

A. Yes, sir.

Q. You are pretty well acquainted with the people here?

A. Yes, sir; I know a good many of the citizens here—did
know them out in the country before the war. I didn't
know many of them in Vicksburg. I lived out in the
country.

Q. You lived up near Snyder's place?

A. Yes, sir.

Q. Own property up there?

A. Yes, sir. My grandfather had a big tract of land up there.[10]

So Calvin Chavis, standing on that stool in the sheriff's office on December 7, 1874, watching the mob intimidate his boss, the elected black sheriff of Warren County, was witness to a pivotal moment in the march by whites to derail the progress of black people toward political equality in Mississippi. Although this incident is not the end of the story—Peter Crosby was reinstated and served as sheriff for a few months longer before being fatally shot in a barroom disagreement by the white deputy who replaced Calvin Chavis—the momentum gained by the Taxpayers' League during the "Vicksburg Troubles" encouraged the withholding of the right of African Americans to vote; this lasted for almost another hundred years, until the Voting Rights Act of 1965. Calvin survived the political difficulties of 1874 and will come back into the story later, but before going into that, we must return to Washington Chavis and the probate of his father's will.

When Washington successfully petitioned to be named administrator of the estate, he listed as assets horses, mules, cows, wagons, farming utensils, and household property valued at about $1,000. Survivors listed are five children: Washington, Preston, Hamilton, Polly (Mary Ann), and Jerusha.[11] However, on learning that Jordan had deeded everything he owned to Jerusha in 1868, therefore leaving no estate, he declined to take out his letters of administration and the matter rested there until 1886, when his son Alexander successfully petitioned to be named administrator of his grandfather's estate in order to reopen the claim denied by the federal government in 1871 for reimbursement for goods taken by the Union army in the summer of 1863.

It should also be noted that it was in 1875 or 1876 when young Albert Gallatin Cason, my future grandfather, climbed into that boxcar headed for Arkansas, to be followed by his mother, Jerusha, his sister Missouri, brother-in-law Osbern Jeffers, and their children. Considering the racial situation in Mississippi, the mid-1870s must have seemed almost as good a time for them to leave Mississippi and become white as 1859 had for Hamilton, Alexander, and Mary Ann.

During the rest of the 1870s Washington and Calvin remained

active in Republican Party politics; but Washington, at least, became so disillusioned with the prospects for African Americans in Mississippi that he thought about going to Kansas with the "Exodusters" in 1879. Here is a letter he wrote to Blanche K. Bruce, the first black man to serve a full term in the US Senate. Omega was the site of the post office on the Louisiana side of the river, opposite Vicksburg. His description of the difference in respect accorded his son Calvin in Illinois, where his visit is noted in the local paper, and in Mississippi, where he is forbidden to go into the white cabin on a steamboat, is poignant testimony to the reality of their situation.

Omega
February 6 1879

Hon B K Bruce Dear Sir after Some time I have the time to drop you a few lines to let you know about the affares in the South the emigration to Kansas is raisen great excitement through all the country if the colored people are well treated thare, will be none of them left in the South in two years. I intend to go with the croud that is going next year if I am liven then the old rebs have very long faceses they Say that they are going to Send to Chinees for labours let them Send to China re ennywhere they pleas the old rebs has too much old prejudice that is bound to Distroy not only the one that has it but it will Distroy both Soul and body and a nation that will let it rule the government and laws of the country they thought when they were righting it around they thought that they were doing big thangs they See now there foly but I think it is too late now for much reforme god has let them go on with there wickedness long a nuff I am glad to See it ended. A Short time Since my son Calvin went up to Ilinois where he was raised the newspapers Commented on his return to his native home but when he came back to Vicksburg he thought he would go up to his plantation on a Steam Boat he went to go through the cabin to the Beuro as they call the Sell where they put the colored people when a colored man go on board of the Steamers in the South the porter came running and toule him he most not go through the hall he went off down the Stars he met the Captain how [who] wanted him to go back upStars but he told the Captain that he was going away and leave them with there Disseptionish principal and go where every man was treated rite and where they had some law. I could tell you of the ignornce of the South for a hole day but I most Come to a Close nothing but remains your most affectionate friend write when you have time

Washington Chavis[12]

Senator Bruce's reply is, as one might predict, circumspect. This is his secretary's copy kept for the files:

> Hon Wash. Chavis
> Vicksburg Miss

Dr Sir.

> Yr letter of [the] 6the inst. is at hand & contents noted. As one of [the] old boys I am always glad to hear from you and know that yr condition is prospering. Sometime since I sent you a quantity of seed which I hope have been rec'd. If they have not been rec'd & it is not too late for planting please notify me & I shall have [the] order duplicated. I shall be glad at all times to forward you such pub. Docs. As may be deemed useful to you & to render you such service here as my position will enable me to do.

> With kind regards to yrself & family
> I am fondly yours
> (sign)[13]

Washington did not join the exodus to Kansas, but thousands justifiably did, according to this quotation from the minority report of the US Senate committee appointed in 1880 to investigate the causes of the mass black migration from the South in the 1870s:

> In the spring of 1879, thousands of colored people unable longer to endure the intolerable hardships, injustice, and suffering inflicted upon them by a class of Democrats in the South, had, in utter despair, fled panic-stricken from their

homes and sought protection among strangers in a strange land. Homeless, penniless, and in rags, these poor people were thronging the wharves of Saint Louis, crowding the steamers on the Mississippi River, and in pitiable destitution throwing themselves upon the charity of Kansas. Thousands more were congregating on the banks of the Mississippi River, hailing the passing steamers, and imploring them for a passage to the land of freedom, where the rights of citizens are respected and honest toil rewarded by honest compensation. The newspapers were filled with accounts of their destitution, and the very air was burdened with the cry of distress from a class of American citizens flying from persecutions which they could no longer endure.[14]

Washington's last listing in the US census, in 1880, shows him living alone in Beat 5, Warren County, Mississippi. He claims to be married, but no wife is listed. Both he and Preston are named on the jury list for Warren County in 1888. However, when Alexander took up Preston's claim against the government in 1886, he described Preston as "deceased." The records for the 1890 census have been destroyed, and Washington does not appear in the 1900 records. His wife, Ann, returned to Illinois at some point and is listed in Carmi Township, White County, Illinois, in the 1900 census in the household of her son-in-law William Harrison and her daughter Parzeda.

Is it the irony of fate or a measure of the success of the civil rights movement of the 1960s that Washington Chavis is now cited on the list of "famous people who were born or died in Warren County" on the current Mississippi Genealogical website?[15]

Three of the children who returned to Mississippi with Washington and Ann in 1871 made names for themselves for different reasons. Calvin and Alexander are the only ones to enter our story in a significant way, Calvin because he followed in his grandfather's footsteps as a planter and because of his political activity. Alexander is useful to us because he reopened the claim against the federal government and so inadvertently provides more information on the family. Their youngest son, Jordan, the first in the family known to have graduated from college, was successful in other interesting venues.

While actively taking part in Republican politics, Calvin made his living by farming on a fairly large scale. He bought some land and rented more, and that he was able to do this speaks well for his reputation and credit. But in January 1877, he was sued in chancery court by a black farming partner named Joseph Hasty, who claimed that in 1875 Calvin, an educated man, had taken advantage of his own illiteracy and ignorance of figures to cheat him. He swore that Chavis had cheated him by pretending they had made less cotton than they actually had. Although Calvin showed his accounts, had the fields independently surveyed to prove they had planted only 47 acres in cotton that produced 42 bales (while Hasty claimed 100 acres that produced 120 bales), and produced a reliable witness in the landowner Mary Blake, who claimed she would not believe Joseph Hasty even under oath, he lost the case on May 29, 1878. He immediately appealed to the Mississippi Supreme Court in October 1878 and won reversal and dismissal of the case on April 21, 1879.[16] However, he asked for no remuneration and received none, and his legal fees were probably horrendous. Although the records show that throughout 1879 and 1880 he continued his farming enterprises, even buying more land, he was in deep financial trouble.

At some point he managed to buy the 1,080-acre plot near Snyder's Bluff that had belonged to his grandfather Jordan and then his aunt Jerusha. On December 14, 1880, he mortgaged this farm for $706 on two notes, one due on December 15, 1880, and the other on December 1, 1881, with the understanding that if the payments were not met, the property would be sold for balance due.[17] Apparently, he could not find the money and the property was advertised to be sold at the courthouse door on January 16, 1882.[18]

The 1910 census lists Calvin Chavis in Carmi Township, White County, Illinois, as a widower, age sixty-eight, unemployed, in the household of his brother-in-law, Arthur West.

It would seem logical that our story of the Chavis family in Mississippi should end here. Jordan Chavis is dead and his children

accounted for. The land is gone; his grandson Calvin, the last Chavis
to own it, has left. We might be justified in thinking that surely by
now we know all we can learn about the Chavis family in Mississippi
between 1829 and 1882. But then, to our surprise, another of Jordan's
grandsons, Washington's son Alexander, steps out of the wings and
carries the narrative a bit further.

In February 1886, the Reverend Alexander Chavis successfully
petitions the US Court of Claims to reopen the cases for reimbursement that Jordan and Preston had lost in 1873 because of doubts
that they were loyal Unionists during the Civil War. The federal
government, defendant in the case, opposes the reopening and vig-
orously denies that loyalty has been proved. Alexander pleads that
his grandfather and uncle were wrongfully accused of disloyalty and
sets out to prove this by producing testimony from new witnesses.
In Jordan's case, the new testimony comes from two prominent
white men in the community; Union men themselves, they swear
that they knew him to have been one as well. Their testimony is
interesting because it comes from neighboring white men, whereas
his witnesses in the first claim filed were former slaves of his, who
were probably still dependent in one way or another, perhaps as his
sharecroppers, and therefore less likely to be objective.[19]

James Stafford testified before J. T. Strother, US commissioner
at Vicksburg, on February 10, 1887:

> I keep a hotel near Vicksburg, have no interest in this claim
> and am not in any way related to the claimant, Jordan Chavis.
> I was personally acquainted with him during the war. He was
> opposed to the rebellion and in favor of the Union during
> the entire war. He was well known as a Union man by his
> expressions and actions. I know to a certainty that he was
> truly loyal. . . . He did not serve in the Confederate militia or
> army or furnish any substitute. . . . In many conversations his
> expressions were always opposed to the success of the South
> and in favor of the Union. I can't remember his words, it was
> so long ago. I heard his neighbors speak of him different ways.
> He was afraid to say anything to secessionists about his senti-
> ments, but to me who he knew was a Union man he would

talk. I do not know that he sold anything to the Confederate Government and never knew or heard of him contributing in any way to the Confederate cause. . . . A nephew of his was in the rebel army. I never heard of him giving him anything. Never knew him to give anything to equip rebel soldiers. If he had I should have known it.[20]

James Fossett, before the same officer at the same time and place, testified as follows:

I am a farmer, 52 years of age and live in Warren County, Mississippi. Am not related to the claimant and have no interest in the claim. I knew Jordan Chavis during the war and knew his sentiments. He was opposed to the war. I don't know how the public regarded him but knew him to be loyal. . . . He was a colored man and it would have resulted likely in his being hung if he had openly spoken in favor of the Union after the war began. I don't suppose he made it a rule to talk his sentiments to his neighbors only to those he [knew] were opposed to the war. He dare not perform loyal acts. He could not show his loyalty by expressions. . . . I did not associate with him as he was not of my color but I knew his sentiments from occasionally meeting him and speaking to him. He did not, to my knowledge furnish the Confederate government any stores or supplies, or make any contract with them, and [I] never heard of his contributing anything to the Confederate cause. . . . I don't know of his having done anything in favor of the Union. He dared not have done so. I heard him speak of his sentiments as opposed to the war.

I saw him three or four times each year . . . probably oftener. I never heard of his having relatives in the Confederate army. I never heard of him contributing anything toward equipment of militia or Confederate soldiers and I should have heard it if he had, as I lived but five miles from him.[21]

One cannot help wondering how it could be that the *Vicksburg Whig* and the *New York Times* knew about that contribution of $500 and a horse to the Confederate cause in June 1861 when

Jordan's neighbors don't seem to have heard about it! At any rate, on January 3, 1888, Jordan Chavis was found by the Court of Claims to have been loyal to the government of the United States throughout the war.

With the loyalty question settled, the case proceeded to an examination of the merits of the claim, and the assistant US attorney general asked that the case be denied on the basis of variations in estimates made in the original testimony by Jordan Chavis and his two former slaves about exactly what was taken by the troops and the value thereof. This argument apparently had some effect because on February 16, 1888, although finding in favor of the claimant, the court awarded only $950 instead of the $2,746 claimed.[22] Surely this is the end of the story, and Alexander received a government check for $950. But this apparently did not happen; the case remained open.

And wait; there's more! On March 30, 1891, the attorney general of the United States, apparently unwilling to give up on this case and using a tactic that he might have been expected to use in the first place, asked the Department of Justice to "transmit certified copies of all accounts, letters, affidavits, records, and of all other papers in the *Confederate* archives touching the question of the loyalty or disloyalty of said Jordan Chavis to the United States Government."[23]

A prompt reply brought a copy of a voucher issued to Jordan Chavis on stationery of *The Confederate States of America*, dated December 26, 1862, for "hauling ammunition from Vicksburg to Snyder's Mills, six-mule team from Dec. 26, 1862 to Jan'y 1st, 1863, 7 days @$6.00 == $42.00."[24] The document was signed by two assistant quartermasters and Jordan Chavis.

The assistant attorney general of the United States, using this voucher as evidence of the claimant's support of the Confederacy and, therefore, his disloyalty to the United States during the war, demanded a new trial. The record of Congressional Case #623 ends here. There is nothing more in Jordan Chavis's file.

As for Preston's reopened case of 1886, on March 28, 1887,

he was found to have been loyal to the United States throughout the war, so a stipulation was entered to proceed to the question of the merits of the claim. But on November 28, 1887, a motion was entered to temporarily withdraw the "Brief on Merits," and on January 2, 1892, he was declared to have been disloyal.[25] This is the last document in the file.

Washington's youngest son, Jordan, who had also returned to Mississippi with his parents in 1870, after attending a private school, entered the brand-new land grant college for African Americans in Mississippi, Alcorn State, in 1872, enrolled in the "Normal" course, and graduated as a teacher in 1876. Shortly after, he was also ordained and preached and taught school for a few years in Mississippi, then in 1880 went north for a distinguished career as a Baptist minister in Illinois. He was the first black man to preach in the State House in Springfield, where his audience consisted of one thousand people.[26] At the rank of captain, he served as chaplain in Cuba in the Eighth Illinois United States Volunteers, the first all-black regiment in the US Army to be led solely by black officers.[27] He was a dedicated Republican and took part in politics in Illinois throughout his life, serving as a delegate in both state and national party conventions.

And so ends our history of Jordan Chavis, his children, and grandchildren in Mississippi. This is the stuff that might have been expected to drift down to our dinner table in stories told by our mother. What did we lose by that silence?

CHAPTER 8

Conclusion:
The Bowl of Rose Leaves

A fter almost ten years of sporadic research and fairly constant rumination, I think that my cousins and I have learned about as much as we can about our Chavis ancestors in Mississippi, and the remaining task will be to find some meaning in the search. As I said in the beginning, the real story here is theirs, and now that we know what it was, we can ask what it has to do with us. Everything I have written about here happened a very long time ago. What difference does it make that there's a new pattern in the family kaleidoscope? Does it signify enough in our lives to make it worth the telling? Would knowing it earlier have made a difference to us and, as I grandly claimed in the beginning, to the life of the nation? We have learned much, much more about "them" than I thought we possibly could, but what does it have to do with "us"?

The answer begins in the unique quality of the story of Jordan Chavis's progress from the frontier in 1829 toward fulfilling what must have been his ambition to become a successful planter by 1861. We have seen that in order to do this, he had to behave like successful planters: he had to acquire land and slaves to work it. And he did this honorably enough to gain the respect and approval of his white neighbors, who thought enough of him to petition the legislature to allow him to remain in Mississippi while passing laws to exile those like him. He, in turn, responded to the crisis of secession by behaving as his white neighbors did. Granted, his later testimony and his actions, governed by expediency, are contradictory. We cannot know what he really thought about the war in his heart of hearts, but his public response was the donation of that

$500 and a horse to the Confederate cause, and his wagons were used to haul munitions for the Rebel army. In other words, in this as in the way he built his business, he behaved much like some of his neighbors who later, in their testimony on his behalf, revealed that although they did not *believe* in the Confederate cause, they had still felt compelled to serve in its army.

On the other hand, in spite of his financial and personal success and his typical patriotic behavior toward the Confederacy, he is still a "colored" man, *not like them*, as far as they are concerned. He is "other." To quote the *New York Times*, "he is spoken of as a 'real bonafide colored man, long well known in this community, who by his correct and honest deportment, has gained the esteem of all who knew him.'" "I did not associate with him as he was not of my color, but I knew his sentiments from occasionally meeting him and speaking to him," a witness to his postwar claim for reimbursement from the government puts it. There is never any question that this man is colored. The public records say so and, after all, one of his sons did free a slave woman, marry her, and return to live in a neighboring county.

And yet at least four of his children are light enough to cross the river and pass for white, which they do with a vengeance. Because obviously they do aspire to be white, for within a couple of years two of his "white" sons and a "white" grandson join the Confederate army as white soldiers in a white regiment. Still, these people, although light enough to pass into the white world, were dark enough, somehow, to be sold into slavery if caught.

So, what did being white mean in 1859 if a light enough colored person could step into it simply by crossing a river? What does it mean now, in 2014? And what, finally, is to be drawn from all this? To what purpose have I disturbed the dust on the bowl of rose leaves?

In the first place, at the personal level, the empty spaces that represented these people in my imagination when I first learned that they had existed have been filled by ghosts as believable to me as the ones from my father's side of the family who seem sometimes to be still in the house. The ancestors who were denied to us, the Chavises, are now people we can imagine as having once been real because we know their predicament, their ambitions and successes as well as failures. We have watched some of them climb the ladder to success and then fall off. We have seen photographs that show what several of them looked like, and from reading some of their personal statements, we can almost hear their voices. They are now part of *our* story, which has expanded to include, among other things, the other side of Reconstruction, the side of it condemned in all the indignant "white" stories we heard about it as children in our house and in school. It turns out that contrary to what we were taught, it was also *our* side that lost in that struggle, with the resultant suppression of the black vote and denial of adequate education for black children in the South for almost a hundred years. We have come to understand that when the kaleidoscope turns, the new pattern it makes is permanent. When a narrative changes, so does the position of the characters in it.

I mentioned at the outset the resemblance of this story to a palimpsest, and it turns out that, as frequently happens, the original text, even in its incomplete, damaged state, is interesting and valuable for interpreting what has been written over it.

Because a deeper level of meaning turned up by this search tells me that what I learned has larger implications than my family's history. I think that if I had heard these stories as a child, my vision of America, the United States, would be different, as would my understanding of my place in it. I believe this because of the change in my vision, experienced on this journey begun in my old age. A remarkable thing happened in my eighty-second year that I will try to explain.

The subtitle of my memoir, *Born in the Delta,* written in 1990, was *Reflections on the Making of a Southern White Identity.* My point in that book was that the culture made one "white." If you were white in color, you were taught to see with white eyes. White eyes see a white world as superior. And, naturally, if you are part of that world it follows that you, too, are superior. I have come to understand that sometimes white eyes, even liberal white eyes, can see the black world intellectually and sympathetically but still, in spite of the best intentions, at some deep atavistic level not comprehend it. I did not come upon this revelation until I was near the end of this research.

In the autumn of 2013, after seven or eight years of thinking about this project, I decided it was time to go down to Mississippi and find the place that Jordan Chavis owned in Warren County. I needed to see what it looked like. Olivia Sordo, my companion, and I drove down the Arkansas side of the Delta to Lake Village, crossed the Mississippi on the new bridge, turned south on old Highway 1, that runs near the river, got off it onto Highway 61 at a place encouragingly named "Onward," and traveled on to Redwood, the largest town near the situation of his farm. The legal description of the property I had taken from the copy of the original deed was easily located on a map, near Ball Ground, five miles northeast of Redwood, on Highway 3 about ten miles north of Vicksburg, as the crow flies.

At Ball Ground we turned right onto Ball Ground Road and headed into woods. The woods got deeper as we drove a mile or two to a point where the blacktop turned to gravel and a little road called Dan Hall Road turned back sharply to the right. Looking at the map, we realized we were either on or very close to what had been Jordan Chavis's land, now completely grown up in impenetrable forest. With the exception of the modern addition of kudzu growing over everything, including trees, and the fact that the regrowth trees are smaller than the originals would have been in 1857, it must look much as it did when he bought it. Remember, then only 120 of the 1,080 acres were listed on the tax record as "improved." And the gullies, visible from the road and now covered with undergrowth and trees, were as formidable as Solon Robinson had described them on his visit to Warren County in 1845. It was hard to imagine this place having been worth the trouble it took to make it profitable, and it was hard to imagine it being between the lines of two raging armies. And yet, the records show that it was. This was where our forefather, Jordan Chavis, after so many years of struggling, reached the apex of his success. *Sic transit gloria mundi.*

We had come prepared to take pictures but there was nothing to photograph but trees. So we drove on to Vicksburg and on the next day visited the Old Court House Museum, where the director, George "Bubba" Bolm, had kindly pulled out some records concerning the Chavis family for me to look through. The museum is situated in the imposing building constructed as the Warren County Courthouse in 1857. When I asked which room would have been Sheriff Peter Crosby's office, I was told it was the room that now houses the library, the very room we were sitting in. So we were looking at those old deeds in the office where in December 1874 Washington's son Calvin Chavis, my grandfather Albert Cason's first cousin, had stood on a stool and watched a mob of white men eject the elected black sheriff of Warren County, the act that essentially marked the beginning of the end of Reconstruction in Mississippi!

There was no plaque commemorating this event, but the very existence of the museum is a monument to it. For this museum is so dedicated to preserving the aura of the Confederacy that the trustees proudly refuse to accept funding from any agency that might object to their "occasional politically incorrect" approach, as the director informed us. It survives on private donations rather than grants from federal and state funding agencies. But making no claim for anything else, the museum is impressive for what it is. The courtroom is intact and there are rooms with case after case filled with authentic antebellum clothing and artifacts. Entering it is like stepping into a trunk full of old things in the attic of a house that has been otherwise empty since 1865.

From there, we drove to Jackson and turned south on the Natchez Trace Parkway because I wanted to travel, as nearly as possible, down part of the road that Jordan Chavis had marched in 1815 and that the family had probably traveled to Claiborne County in 1828 or so. While not built strictly on the old Natchez Trace, the modern highway follows it in places and for the entire span runs in a strip of well-managed forest that in its closed-in state must give some inkling of what it might have been like 185 years ago. There is nothing but the road; you cannot see through the woods on either side to the surrounding fields. It is a daunting prospect to imagine traveling almost four hundred miles over it in all weathers, closed in by the woods so that there are no horizons, eaten up by mosquitoes and flies, constantly fearing wild animals and bandits, in wagons full of children and all of a family's possessions, pulled by mules or oxen frequently through deep mud, making seven miles on good days, fewer on bad ones.

We ended the southward journey at Natchez, a town deservedly renowned for the beauty and grace of its antebellum homes. During trips to Natchez several times before, dazzled by their elegance, I had enjoyed touring the interiors of those houses and their grounds. But this time, from the very beginning, I felt something different about the way I found myself looking at their carefully preserved splendor. Olivia, who had been there with me on earlier occasions, remarked on this difference; something seemed wrong. I had no desire to go inside any of them, to get any closer than driving down the street. Later, I realized that the difference was this: I could no longer compartmentalize; I could no longer separate the architectural beauty and grace from the human misery it had taken to achieve it. For the first time, when I looked at those mansions, I thought to myself, "The people who had all this built were not my tribe." I found myself remarking to Olivia that while every crumbling brick in every sinking garden walk was being restored, the shotgun houses that told another story about Natchez were being allowed to fall down. I think for the first time in my life the enormity of slavery and its aftermath came down on me. Before, I realized now, the guilt I had experienced, in spite of my best intentions, was so detached as to be almost an *observation* of guilt. That guilt had been *about me and my discomfort, not concern about them.* For the first time, I found myself wondering what the slaves must have thought about this splendor; when I tried to imagine what African Americans think about it now, I almost thought *we.* I had lost my "white eyes."

And there's irony, of course, in the fact that I could have this response since, in my case, it was exactly the ambition of my colored Mississippi forebears to have one of those mansions, to belong to "that tribe," to be as "white" as possible to avoid being condemned by a slight coloration to lesser achievements and the indignities of an inferior status. For that is part of what it meant to be white in the United States in the mid-nineteenth century.

And this whole narrative is fraught with ironies. Members of my generation and our children, in reference to my father's family, like many other descendants of slave owners, have always felt a certain amount of hereditary guilt. There is no question in our minds that even three or four generations down, we have profited from slavery. And yet, as this study shows, even some of our "colored" ancestors were slave owners, because slavery was an essential part of the economic and social machinery that built our country.

So is our guilt compounded because we get it from both sides? Or should we comfort ourselves with the knowledge that this entire nation from the very beginning and right down to the present day has been complicit in profiting from the institution of slavery and its aftermath? For the record, there's no comfort in it.

Curious about the meaning of "white" today, in 2014, I decided to ask younger members of the family how they were affected by learning of their African ancestry and received some interesting answers that are very encouraging for the hope they hold out for the future of this country as an egalitarian society. Their most common response indicated that they found it merely interesting, a far cry from responses I got from older relatives. From what our children and grandchildren tell me, there has been a seismic shift in the matter of attitudes toward race relations in the United States in the last fifty years. Many maintain that learning of their African American heritage had no effect whatsoever on their perception of themselves and their society. They assure me that in addition to having been taught by their parents to respect everyone, integration of the schools and workplaces has put them so much in contact on an equal level with African Americans and other minorities that they are virtually colorblind. Others tell of feeling initial shock and then subsequent acceptance of the idea. Here are excerpts from some of their responses:

I know my thoughts and ideas changed. I felt funny at first knowing and coming to grips with being part black. These were the people my relatives and parents looked at as being inferior and this helped form my own prejudice. Now I find out I am part of that group. But discovering that the Chavises were smart and talented and had served their country in every war changed my mind a lot. They were such good solid people. I too stopped looking through the veil of my white eyes. (Will Franklin)

The revelation about our ancestry was not really as much a "shock" as it was interesting, but it provoked quite a bit of thought and one of my conclusions is that I feel more American because of it. Previously I was aware of Scots, German, Welsh, Irish, Swiss roots, now I've got to add African. (Eric Bolsterli)

My career was spent in education with a short time in the mental health field. Both of these fields require you to be color blind. And I feel that I was. My prejudices are not toward color, but toward ignorance, love of ignorance, white trash behavior, refusing to see how your behavior affects your children, endless adolescence, me first attitude, disdain of education, religious intolerance, uncivilized behavior and bad manners. (Melinda Holder)

I can honestly say that finding out about the mixture of race in the family has no effect on my feelings. I am who I am because of the battles and struggles of my ancestors. I do feel a great sadness for these ancestors when I think of the struggles and fear they had to endure because of the color of their skin. I am not prejudiced regarding race; I am prejudiced against people who do not take care of their families, regardless of race. I am ashamed to say that in this matter, in the last years of teaching I have found it is the white race that disappoints me most. . . . We have several relatives, on my husband's side I would not let in our house. One has done prison time for manufacturing meth. One has stolen jewelry from our house, my mother-in-law's house and everywhere she has ever been. He has another cousin we think has run drugs from Mexico to Michigan. We have conversations as to what we would do if they appeared at our house and the plan is to act like we are not home! So if these newfound relatives are fine, upstanding folks, I say, "Welcome to the family!" (Robin Looney)

When we were having so much trouble with our health this past year I had as many black friends come into my home and offer to help in any way as white ones. They cleaned up the fallen limbs from my pecan trees and brought meals for two straight months. Black and white friends. I can never repay them. (Bill Lloyd)

I was shocked as I had no idea! I had somewhat of a lily white upbringing with both sides of the family having origins in the South. They had biased and prejudiced ways of dealing with other races. . . . No-one would ever have guessed the African connections in my family. I'm still rethinking the connection myself. It's not helpful at this stage to try to fit in with black folks although I feel a new interest and love for them. . . . The few times I've mentioned it to them it basically has brought on extended, understandable yawns. (Donna Preston)

My first reaction was that—of course—as we are all connected if we look far enough and we are all in this world together. My second reaction was that I felt more of an American than I had thirty seconds before and third, I was excited to learn more. . . . The discovery was actually liberating to me in a way that is often found with the truth. But did it really change me or the way I think? Why would it? I would hope not. My parents did their best to raise me to understand that all people are equal, period, and should be given respect and kindness. I have tried hard to do so and provide some guidance to our children. (Jerry Jones)

I don't think this knowledge has changed my perception of myself and my family except to add to the many reasons I am

proud to be in this family. I have, however wondered if my
Grandfather Jones would have married my grandmother Zena
Cason if he had known she had black ancestors. Times were
different back then; people were not so tolerant.... I did have
a bit of a hard time when my daughter wanted to date a black
boy. We went to counseling together and worked this out. I
think what I mainly objected to was the character of the boy,
not that he was black. If he had been white and didn't have a
job or any ambition, I wouldn't have been too happy about
that choice either. (Lorri Daniels)

It gave me better self-identification; it made me feel more
complete. It made me proud that my family accepts diversity,
that we are very accepting. Many of my friends are African
Americans and I have mostly dated black guys. (Jamie Daniels)

I have been so interested in learning about my mixed ancestry. For the first time in my employment history I have many
black coworkers and it has been interesting to see their sim-
ilarities/non-similarities with me that are just like my white
coworkers. I try not to be prejudiced. I am more drawn to
people by the way they handle themselves and by their character than by their color. (Barbara Staples)

I was born and raised in a small town in Alaska.... [T]here was
one black woman in Anchor Point but there were no African
American children my age.... Even in Alaska there was some
racism imbedded in the language and attitudes when I was
growing up in the 1960's.... There were derogatory names
for the Native Americans and we told and laughed at the
racist jokes du jour—whether about blacks, Chinese, Italians,
Poles or Mexicans. I dated an Alaskan Native girl a few times
and since going outside to college have made friends and
professional associates of various ethnic backgrounds. My first
roommate at the University of Oregon was a Chinese kid
from Hawaii and I had two black roommates in the dorms
at the University of Arkansas and we got along just fine.... I
don't think the confirmation (of African ancestry) has changed

my life or any of my attitudes, nor would it have changed much in my upbringing. I appreciate knowing the facts of my ancestry and know that it made a huge difference seventy-five years ago! (Sam Cason)

These are encouraging answers from individuals to a specific question, but not only did several of them not respond at all, I am well aware that if they had, I might have received discouraging replies as well.

I had to wonder how the descendants of Jordan Chavis who went north, Washington's children and their children, our African American cousins, have fared over the years. Limited, perhaps, by the vestiges of my white upbringing and hence my white vision, even when I set out to learn about the origins of my family I saw it from "our" perspective, but I wondered about the others. We were white because our great-grandparents made the choice to cross the river and pass into the white world, where our grandparents and parents "married white." But what about the others, the ones who "went north" in 1857?

So I was very pleased when, toward the end of research for this project, Will Franklin put me in touch with two of Washington's descendants, Kathy Lawrence and Jennifer Sands-Congleton, great-great-granddaughters of Parzeda Chavis Harrison, Washington's daughter. They were kind enough to answer some questions for me.

The first thing I wanted to know was whether they had been as ignorant of our existence as we were of theirs. Had there been talk in their side of the family, down through the years, about the relatives who had "passed" into the white world? Indeed there had. According to Kathy,

> My grandmother knew all about her relatives and she told all of her children and grandchildren too. So, yes we were all aware of the "white" side of the family that passed. She and her sister Virginia were raised by Parzeda.
> ... I remember my grandmother saying that with some of the family it was a conscious effort to pass. They eventually married white and continued until they "cleaned" their lines

of anything resembling people of color. I remember a story she told of a cousin who passed as white. She had red hair and green eyes. She got pregnant with twins and one came out looking white and of course, one was black. Her husband had no clue that she had black in her and he left her in the hospital!

Another story my grandmother would tell was about Thanksgiving dinner. She said they had big, elaborate dinners and it would look as if the United Nations was sitting at the table: Black, Indian, Irish, Spanish, etc. This was in Carmi, Illinois.

Kathy's grandmother, Betty, is the little girl standing in front in the photograph of Parzeda and her daughter-in-law's family, the Marshalls, included in this book. And therein lies a story that helps illuminate the pain associated with the questions of color in the family. Parzeda's son Jordan married a Native American woman named Irene Marshall, who died when their two daughters were very small. Parzeda stepped in to raise the two children, who were dark in complexion. Her son Elmer, who was light in color, said to his mother, "If you raise those 'nigger' children in this house I will never come home again." And after that, he never visited his mother before dark because he didn't want to be seen going into the house. He did not even attend her funeral.

As a matter of interest, another descendant of that Marshall family, Thurgood, came to national attention as a leading attorney in the civil rights movement and then as the first African American US Supreme Court justice.

Jennifer Sands-Congleton, Elmer Chavis's great-great-granddaughter, offered the following testament to some of that family's internal conflict in the matter of color.

> Because my complexion is a light olive, I can never claim the struggles of a darker skinned African American. However, I will relate what I know about my father and family members' struggles relating to this issue. My father was murdered when I was only five years old. . . . My mother told me that my father was ashamed of being so dark. He did not like to

be out in the sun because he "blackened" so quickly. When
together, they looked like Ebony and Ivory. . . . My grandmother, Gertrude, was married to George Said, also known
as Akil Hussein Abdallah, who was born in Lebanon in 1900
and was very racist against black people. That racism has been
handed down from generation to generation on the Lebanese
side of the family.

Jennifer ended her note to me with a reiteration of her
great-great-grandfather Elmer's threat to stop visiting his mother,
Parzeda, if she took those dark children in to raise with her own
plaintive statement, "What is worse than being a racist against your
own kind?" I suspect that if the whole truth were told, this applies
to more Americans than anyone dreams of. The experience of that
other side of this family underscores the pain and corrosive effect
that the matter of race has caused this entire society.

There could be another book here concerning Washington's
descendants, but I'm not the one who can write it. I have neither
the credentials nor time left in which to do it.

So after this voyage of discovery concerning one American
family tree in this tiny corner of an enormous picture, we are still
faced with the larger question of what "white" means in the United
States now, in 2014. When we have an African American president,
African Americans in Congress and on the US Supreme Court,
and African Americans holding important positions in all the professions, business, and industry as well, obviously, one no longer has
to be white to rise in the public hierarchy of America. And yet, the
path to success for minorities is still so much more difficult, and the
question of the significance of "whiteness" remains. Because there
can be no doubt that, on the whole, it is still terribly significant and
that therein lies "the heart of darkness" in American culture.

It seems that I am ending this study with as many queries as I
had at the beginning. But they are different questions, and that may
be why it was worth the trouble "to disturb the dust on the bowl
of roses."

As for my personal journey, there's something else I have
noticed: not always, but sometimes when people near my age ask

me what I have been working on and I tell them, people I have known for years, both black and white, all liberals of the first order, show not only surprise and shock, but a change in their perception of me. There is a click. The pattern in the kaleidoscope through which they have always looked at *me* has suddenly shifted. There is a moment of embarrassment; they don't know where to go with this, what to say next. My cultural background is what it has always been; my skin is as white as always, but suddenly I am not who they thought I was. And I have the feeling that the shock comes not so much from hearing there was miscegenation in my family between 300 and 150 years ago, but from the fact that I am *telling* it.

And they are right of course. There is a difference: I am not who they thought I was. I am not even who I thought I was. I no longer have "white eyes."

Tax Records Quoted in Chapter 3

The 1830 Claiborne County tax roll lists Jordan Chavis as "Col'd." and his situation is Chuby's York, 1 free person of color, with tax due: $3.30.[1]

The 1831 Claiborne County tax roll finds him much the same except with a new situation, Brocus Creek. He is "Colored," 1 free person of color, with tax due: $3.00.[2]

His assessment for 1832 cannot be found, but his finances have taken a turn for the better by 1833, when his entry reads: "Col'd." and his situation is Brocus Creek, 1 free person of color, 2 slaves, aged between 5 and 60, and tax due: $3.00.[3]

Ownership of slaves shows him on an upward track toward prosperity, which he is able to maintain. For in 1836, while still living on Brocus Creek in Claiborne County, Jordan Chavis buys 403 acres of land for $4,000 in adjacent Jefferson County.[4]

In 1838, he is listed in the Jefferson County tax rolls as living on Clarke's Creek, 2 free persons of color, 3 slaves, aged between 5 and 60, and tax due: $7.87.[5] In 1840 he is listed in the US census in Jefferson County as head of a household that includes seven free persons of color and two slaves. In the tax rolls he is listed without racial designation and assesses 460 acres of land, "class 4-quality 1. Clarks Cr.," 1 free person of color, 2 slaves, aged between 5 and 60, with tax due: $7.70.[6]

In the 1846 Jefferson County tax rolls he is listed heading a household with 1 free person of color, 7 slaves, tax due: $5.80.[7]

In the 1850 US census he is listed for the first time as "Planter," with real estate valued at $720, in Township 9 East, Jefferson County, Mississippi, mulatto, head of household #362 with Mary A. Saucer, mulatto (his daughter), John Saucer, mulatto (son-in-law), J. Casen, mulatto (his daughter), and Missouri Casen, mulatto (Jerusha's daughter). His age is listed as 53.[8]

In the "Slave Schedule" he is listed with ownership of ten slaves.

In the "Agriculture Schedule," he lists 40 acres improved, 200 acres unimproved, value $720. Value of farming implements is $10, and he has 3 horses, 7 "milch" cows, 6 working oxen, 7 other cattle, 15 swine, with the value of livestock at $395. He also has 500 bushels of corn, 9 bales of ginned cotton, 50 bushels of peas and beans, 260 bushels of sweet potatoes, and 100 pounds butter.

On September 1, 1851, Jordan buys another 40 acres of land in Jefferson County, from the government this time.[9]

Jordan's son Washington also buys 40 acres of government land in Jefferson County in April 1851.[10]

By 1853, Jordan Chavis is living in Warren County, where he is listed on the tax rolls as a free man of color with 11 slaves, 1 stallion, 8 mares, and 37 bales of cotton. He seems to be on the way from being a "farmer" to becoming a "planter," as the census taker had already categorized him in 1850.[11]

On March 27, 1857, Jordan Chavis buys 1,080 acres of land in Warren County from Joseph and Pauline Parks for $1,400.[12]

In 1858, his son Preston buys 107 acres in Warren County at the courthouse door for $345.[13]

In the 1860 agriculture census for Warren County, Jordan and Preston are listed next to each other and both seem to be farming Jordan's large plot because each lists about half the acreage of that 1,080-acre farm.

Jordan lists 150 improved acres, 450 unimproved, value of land at $1,000, and the value of implements at $200; he has 2 horses, 3 mules, 13 milk cows, 10 oxen, 50 other cattle, 10 swine, and the value of livestock is $300. He also has 300 bushels of corn, 50 bushels of peas and beans, 20 bushels of Irish potatoes, 200 bushels of sweet potatoes, 500 pounds of butter. Value of homemade manufactures is $100. Value of animals slaughtered is $50.[14]

The "Slave Schedule" lists 10 slaves for him and ten slave houses.[15]

Preston lists 40 acres improved, 450 unimproved, with the value of $800. Implements are worth $100; he has 3 horses, 3 mules, 3 milk cows, 20 other cows, 25 swine, and the value of the livestock is $1,000. He also has 300 bushels of corn, 50 bushels of peas and beans, 25 bushels of Irish potatoes, 250 bushels of sweet potatoes, 500 pounds of butter. Value of homemade manufactures is $100. Value of animals slaughtered is $50.[16]

NOTES

CHAPTER 2
Jordan Chavis Establishes Himself in Mississippi

1. See www.nytreprints.com. Copyright 2012, The New York Times Company. This article was picked up by other northern papers, including *The Sentinel*, June 27, 1861, in Keene, New Hampshire.

2. *Vicksburg Weekly Citizen*, May 6, 1861.

3. *Vicksburg Weekly Herald*, June 24, 1861.

4. Quoted in "Brief on Loyalty," Jordan Chavis, Admin. Vs The United States, in the Court of Claims, Cong. No. 623, December term, 1886. (In a refiling of the original 1871 petition by his grandson Alexander Chavis.)

5. Marlboro County Estates, Apt 8, Package 15, Aquilla Quick, South Carolina Archives, microfilm C1612.

6. Heinegg, *Free African Americans*, 1:7.

7. Ibid.

8. Sharfstein, *The Invisible Line*, 20–21.

9. Ibid., 62.

10. Ibid., 10.

11. See Berlin, *Slaves without Masters*.

12. Bounty Land Warrant: 26075, US National Archives and Records Administration, Washington, DC (hereafter cited as NARA).

13. Ibid.

14. Claiborne County Tax Rolls, 1820–1841, Box 3621, image 151 of 601, Familysearch.com.

15. Marlboro County Estates, Apt 8, Package 15, Aquilla Quick; Marlboro County, *Deed Book H-1*, 63–87, South Carolina Archives, microfilm C1541.

16. *Fourth Census of the United States, 1820*, Records of the Bureau of the Census, RG 29, microfilm publication M33, 142 rolls, NARA. See also Ancestry. com; 1820 United States Federal Census database online.

17. Familysearch.com, Claiborne County Tax Rolls, 1820–1841, Box 3621, image 151 of 601.

18. Sydnor, "The Free Negro in Mississippi before the Civil War," 786.

19. Ibid., 770–71.

20. Ibid., 780.

21. Hogan and Davis, *William Johnson's Natchez*, 53–54.

22. Buckingham, *The Slave States of America*, 479–80.

23. Robinson, "Notes of Travel in the Southwest," 1:458.

24. Olmsted, *A Journey in the Back Country*, 1:178.

25. Robinson, "Visit to Warren County," 2:476 and 478.

26. See Anderson, *Brokenburn*, throughout.

CHAPTER 3

Jordan Chavis's Farming Operations in Mississippi, 1830–1860

1. I am indebted to Sue Moore, a historian of Claiborne County, for this information about the mulatto slaveholders in Claiborne and Jefferson Counties. Her white ancestors, David Herlong and wife, Mary Varnardo, owned the plantation nearest the "Holly Group."

2. *Fifth Census of the United States, 1830*, Records of the Bureau of the Census, RG 29, microfilm publication M19, 201 rolls, NARA. See also Ancestry.com; 1820 United States Federal Census database online.

3. For more complete records, see the appendix.

4. "Schedule 1, Free Inhabitants, Jefferson County, Mississippi," *Seventh United States Census, 1850*, NARA.

5. "Schedule 4, Production of Agriculture in Warren County, 1860," 11. For detailed information, see appendix.

6. "Schedule 2, Slave Inhabitants in the County of Warren, State of Mississippi," *1860 US Federal Census*, p. 71, Ancestry.com.

7. Robinson, "Visit to Warren County," 2:446.

CHAPTER 4

The Chavis Children, 1830–1860

1. There is another possible, very puzzling connection between the Vause and Chavis families in a deed recorded June 29, 1838, showing that a Mary Chavis bought a six-year-old slave boy named Levi from W. G. Vause for $500 on condition that she would free him on November 9, 1856, when he would be twenty-five years old. Jordan's daughter Mary Ann would have been twenty-three at this time. This could not be her child as he would be free because she is free. He never shows up again. What is going on here? Jefferson County, *Deed Book D*, page 41, Mississippi Department of Archives and History, Jackson (hereafter cited as MDAH).

2. "Records of Free and Freed African Americans, Massac County, Illinois," *The Saga of Southern Illinois* 27 (Summer 2000): 27. (According to the archivist at the Illinois State Archives, who provided this copy, the original document has been misplaced.)

3. "Schedule 1, Free Inhabitants, Copiah County, Mississippi," *Seventh United States Census, 1850*, Ancestry.com.

4. "Schedule 2, Slave Inhabitants, Copiah County, Mississippi," *Seventh United States Census, 1850*, Ancestry.com.

5. "Schedule 4, Agriculture Schedule, Copiah County, Mississippi," *Seventh United States Census, 1850*, Ancestry.com.

6. Widow No. 10363, Mexican War, General Affidavits of Abigail Bowie and Sallie Branch, Department of the Interior, Bureau of Pensions, Washington, DC.

7. "Schedule 1, Free Inhabitants, Warren County, Mississippi," *Seventh United States Census, 1850*, Ancestry.com.

8. Warren County Tax Rolls, 1850, Box 29678, Image 3 of 18, Mississippi State Archives, Jackson, Various Records, 1820–1951, familysearch.com.

9. See Weaver, *Mississippi Farmers, 1850–1860*, 124–25.

CHAPTER 5

Years of Hope/Years of Despair: The Chavis Family in the 1850s

1. Berlin, *Slaves without Masters*, 344–45.

2. Ibid., 373.

3. Morris, *Becoming Southern*, 175.

4. *Servitude Detailed Information*, Illinois State Archives, Springfield, ilsos.gov/isa/servEman.Search.do?nameNo3380,3378,3377,3379,3381.

5. "Records of Free African Americans, Massac County, Illinois," *The Saga of Southern Illinois* 27, no. 2 (Summer 2000): 25–26 (Genealogy Society of Southern Illinois, Carterville).

6. Gertz, "The Black Laws of Illinois," 466.

7. *1860 United States Census*, "Population Schedule," Township 16SRange5E, Massac, Illinois, Roll M653_209, page 823, Image 27, Family History Library Film 803209, Ancestry.com.

8. *Weekly Vicksburg Whig*, December 7, 1859.

9. Ibid., December 14, 1859.

10. Ashley County, *Deed Book C*, 67, Ashley County Courthouse, Hamburg, Arkansas.

11. US General Land Office Records, 1796–1907, Hamilton H. Chavis and Alexander B. Chavis, Ancestry.com.

12. RG 47, Series 2370, Box 14, 128, MDAH.

CHAPTER 6

War and Its Aftermath for the Chavis Family, 1861–1873

1. RG 123, US Court of Claims, Cong. #623, Jordan Chavis, tabbed, Box 133, 16E3/08/17/01, NARA. The other quotes in this section are also from this source.

2. RG 123, US Court of Claims, Cong. #623, Jordan Chavis.

3. Records of Fisher Funeral Home, Vicksburg, Mississippi, 1871–1874, copied and alphabetized by Mary Lois Sheffield Ragland, August, September, October 1986, Old Court House Museum, Vicksburg.

4. RG 123, US Court of Claims, Cong. #571, Preston Chavis, tabbed, Box 124, 16E3/08/16/06, NARA.

5. Ibid.

6. Currie, *Enclave: Vicksburg and Her Plantations*, 67.

7. Warren County, *Deed Book EE*, 148.

8. Warren County, *Deed Book FF*, 278.

9. Ibid., 306.

10. "List of Errors, Insolvent and Delinquent Tax Payers, Warren County, Mississippi for the Fiscal Year ending May A. D., 1868," Insolvent, Delinquent, and Other Tax Lists (Warren County), Series 341, Box 30043, B1/R34/B3/S1, MDAH.

11. Warren County, *Deed Book HH (1869–1870)*, 301.

12. 1870 Census: Township 16, Range 5, Massac, Illinois, Roll M593-295, Page 285B, Image 578, Family History Library Film: 54574, Ancestry.com.

13. Warren County, *Deed Book LL*, 320.

14. Warren County, *Deed Book HH*, 249.

15. *1870 United States Census*, "Population Schedule, Milldale, Warren, Mississippi," Roll: M593–751, Page: 158B, Image: 320, Family History Library Film: 552250, Ancestry.com.

16. *1870 United States Census, Agriculture Census*, "Schedule 3, Oak Ridge Mississippi," Ancestry.com.

17. "List of Insolvent & Delinquent Taxes, Warren County, 1871," Series 341, Box 3887, B21/R93/B81/S1, MDAH.

CHAPTER 7

Reconstruction and Ruin, 1873–1882

1. McLemore, *A History of Mississippi*, 583 ff.

2. Ibid., 586.

3. Lemann, *Redemption*, 86.

4. Ibid., 83–89.

5. Foner, *Reconstruction*, 558–59.

6. "Testimony Taken before the Vicksburgh Investigating Committee," *Reports of Committees of The House of Representatives for the Second Session of the Forty-Third Congress, 1874–75*, vol. 1.

7. Ibid., 385–86.

8. Ibid., 389.

9. Ibid., 390.

10. Ibid., 387.

11. Chancery Court Records, Warren County, File 2841, p. 290, Probate, April 8, 1874, MDAH.

12. Blanche K. Bruce Papers, Howard University, Washington, DC.

13. Ibid.

14. "Report and Testimony of the Select Committee of the United States Senate to Investigate the Cause of the Removal of the Negroes from the Southern States to the Northern States," 46th Cong., 2nd sess., 1880, S. Rep 693 (3 parts) p. x, NARA. Quoted in Damani Davis, "Exodus to Kansas," 2008, www.archives.gov/publications/prologue/2008/summer/exodus.html.

15. See http://warren.msgenweb.org/Notables.htm.

16. Warren County Chancery Court, Joseph Hasty vs Calvin Chavis, #2897, May 29, 1878, Box 5949, B2-R123, B9–55, MDAH.

17. Warren County, *Deed Book YY*, 431.

18. *Vicksburg Daily Commercial*, December 31, 1881.

19. RG 123, US Court of Claims, Cong. #623, Jordan Chavis, tabbed, Box 133, 16E3/08/17/01, Alex Chavis Adm of Jordan Chavis Est, Miss. vs. The United States, NARA.

20. Ibid.

21. Ibid.

22. RG 123, Bowman Act—Facts and Loyalty, US Court of Claims, Cong. #623, Alex Chavis Admr. Vs. The United States, Findings of Fact, NARA.

23. RG 123, H. R. 7616, Department of Justice, Letter to Secretary of War, March 30, 1891, NARA.

24. RG 123, 6943, Archive Office, War Department, June 30, 1876, Book 3, Letters Sent, p. 175, Case of Jordan Chavis, Warren Co., Miss., Bill and voucher for hauling ammunition, NARA.

25. RG 123, US Court of Claims, Cong. #571, Preston Chavis, tabbed, Box 124, 16E3/08/16/06, NARA.

26. *Portrait and Biographical Record of Adams County, Illinois* (Chicago: Chapman Bros., 1892).

27. McCord and Turley, *History of the Eighth Illinois United States Volunteers.*

Appendix

Tax Records Quoted in Chapter 3

1. Claiborne County Tax Rolls, 1820–1841, Box 3621, image 169 of 601, Familysearch.com.

2. Ibid., image 6 of 25.

3. Ibid., image 204 of 601.

4. Jefferson County, *Deed Book C (1837)*, 505.

5. Jefferson County, Tax Rolls, Box 3667, image 8 of 35, Familysearch.com.

6. Ibid., image 7 of 25.

7. Ibid., image 4 of 20.

8. "Schedule 1, Free Inhabitants, Jefferson County, Mississippi," *Seventh United States Census, 1850.*

9. Bureau of Land Management, General Land Office Records, Accession no. MS0490-.068, www.glorecords.blm.gov/.

10. Ibid., Accession no. MS0480-.377.

11. Personal Tax Rolls for Warren County, Mississippi, 1853, Old Court House Museum, Vicksburg. It should be noted that Jonathan Beasley misquoted this source as saying that Jordan Chavis owned 20 slaves in 1853 in his article "Blacks—Slave and Free—Vicksburg, 1850–1860," in the *Journal of Mississippi History* 38, no. 1 (February 1976): 15–16. The mistake was then quoted by John Hebron Moore in *The Emergence of the Cotton Kingdom* as evidence that Jordan Chavis was "the wealthiest free black in Warren County." The mistake was made because the left- and right-hand pages of the record book are not lined up accurately. Correctly aligned, the record shows 11 slaves. However, Chavis may have been the wealthiest free-colored man in Warren County anyway.

12. Warren County, *Deed Book AA*, 1857, 112.

13. Ibid., 1858, 610.

14. "Schedule 4, Production of Agriculture in Warren County, 1860," 11.

15. "Schedule 2, Slave Inhabitants in the County of Warren, State of Mississippi, 1860," 71.

16. Ibid.

BIBLIOGRAPHY

ARTICLES AND CHAPTERS

Beasley, Jonathan. "Blacks—Slave and Free—Vicksburg 1850–1860." *Journal of Mississippi History* 38, no. 1 (February 1976): 1–32.

Gertz, Elmer. "The Black Laws of Illinois." *Journal of Illinois State Historical Society* 56 (Autumn 1963): 454–473.

"Records of Free African Americans, Massac County, Illinois." *The Saga of Southern Illinois* 27, no. 2 (Summer 2000): 25–28. (Genealogy Society of Southern Illinois, Carterville.)

Robinson, Solon. "Notes of Travel in the Southwest—No. VI." In *Solon Robinson Pioneer and Agriculturist, Selected Writings*, ed. Herbert Anthony Kellar. Vol. 1, *1825–1845*. (Indiana Historical Bureau, Indianapolis, 1936, vol. 21, openlibrary.org.)

———. "Visit to Warren County—Vicksburg—Hillside cultivation—Orcharding—etc." In *Solon Robinson Pioneer and Agriculturist, Selected Writings*, ed. Herbert Anthony Kellar. Vol. 2, *1846–1851*. (Indiana Historical Bureau, Indianapolis, 1936, vol. 22, openlibrary.org.)

Sydnor, Charles. "The Free Negro in Mississippi before the Civil War." *American Historical Review* 32, no. 4 (July 1927): 786.

BOOKS

Anderson, John Q., ed. *Brokenburn: The Journal of Kate Stone, 1861–1868*. Baton Rouge: Louisiana State University Press, 1972.

Berlin, Ira. *Slaves without Masters: The Free Negro in the Antebellum South*. New York: New Press, 1975.

Buckingham, J. S. *The Slave States of America*. London: Fisher & Co., 1842. Online: archive.org.

Currie, James T. *Enclave: Vicksburg and Her Plantations, 1863–1870*. Jackson: University Press of Mississippi, 1980.

Foner, Eric. *Reconstruction: America's Unfinished Revolution, 1863–1877*. New York: Harper & Row, 1988.

Heinegg, Paul. *Free African Americans of North Carolina, Virginia, and South Carolina from the Colonial Period to about 1820*. Vol. 1. Baltimore: Clearfield Company, 2005.

Hogan, William Ransom, and Edwin Adams Davis. *William Johnson's Natchez*. Baton Rouge: Louisiana State University Press, 1993.

Lemann, Nicholas. *Redemption: The Last Battle of the Civil War*. New York: Farrar, Straus and Giroux, 2006.

McCord, Harry Stanton, and Henry Turley. *History of the Eighth Illinois United States Volunteers*. Chicago: E. F. Harman & Co., 1892. (University of Illinois, Urbana, online catalog.)

McLemore, Richard Aubrey. *A History of Mississippi*. Jackson: University and College Press of Mississippi, 1973.

Moore, John Hebron. *The Emergence of the Cotton Kingdom in the Old Southwest: Mississippi, 1770–1860*. Baton Rouge: Louisiana University Press, 1987.

Morris, Christopher. *Becoming Southern: The Evolution of a Way of Life, Warren County and Vicksburg, Mississippi, 1770–1860*. New York: Oxford University Press, 1995.

Olmsted, Frederick Law. *A Journey in the Back Country*. Vol. 1. New York: G. P. Putnam's Sons and The Knickerbocker Press, 1907.

Portrait and Biographical Record of Adams County, Illinois. Chicago: Chapman Bros., 1892. Online: archive.org.

Sharfstein, Daniel J. *The Invisible Line: Three American Families and the Secret Journey from Black to White*. New York: Penguin Press, 2011.

Walker, Peter F. *Vicksburg: A People at War, 1860–1865*. Chapel Hill: University of North Carolina Press, 1960.

Weaver, Herbert. *Mississippi Farmers, 1850–1860*. Nashville: Vanderbilt University Press, 1945.

DEEDS

Ashley County, Arkansas. *Deed Book C*. Ashley County Courthouse, Hamburg, Arkansas.

Jefferson County, Mississippi. *Deed Book C (1837)*, 505. Mississippi Department of Archives and History, Jackson.

———. *Deed Book D*, 41. Mississippi Department of Archives and History, Jackson.

Marlboro County, South Carolina. *Deed Book H-1*, 63–87 microfilm C1541. South Carolina Archives, Columbia.

Warren County, Mississippi. *Deed Book AA, 1857*, 112. Mississippi Department of Archives and History, Jackson.

———. *Deed Book AA, 1858*, 112. Mississippi Department of Archives and History, Jackson .

———. *Deed Book C (1837)*, 505. Mississippi Department of Archives and History, Jackson .

———. *Deed Book EE*, 148. Mississippi Department of Archives and History, Jackson.

————. *Deed Book FF*, 278. Mississippi Department of Archives and History, Jackson.

————. *Deed Book HH (1869–1870)*, 249. Mississippi Department of Archives and History, Jackson .

————. *Deed Book HH*, 301. Mississippi Department of Archives and History, Jackson.

————. *Deed Book LL*, 320. Mississippi Department of Archives and History, Jackson.

FEDERAL CLAIMS AND REPORTS

Census records. Ancestry.com and familysearch.com.

RG 123, US Court of Claims, Cong. #623, Jordan Chavis. Box 133, 16E3/08/17/01. National Archives and Records Administration, Washington, DC.

RG 123, US Court of Claims, Cong. #571, Preston Chavis. Box 124, 16E/08/16/06. National Archives and Records Administration, Washington, DC.

Testimony Taken before the Vicksburgh Investigating Committee. *Reports of Committees of the House of Representatives for the Second Session of the Forty-third Congress, 1874–1875.*Vol. 1. Washington, DC: Government Printing Office, 1875. (Digitized by Google.)

Widow No. 10363. Mexican War. General Affidavits of Abigail Bowie and Sallie Branch. Bureau of Pensions, Department of the Interior, Washington, DC.

NEWSPAPERS

New York Times. June 21, 1861. (nytreprints.com.)

Port Gibson Reveille. April 1859.

Vicksburg Weekly Citizen. May 6, 1861. Mississippi Department of Archives and History, Jackson.

Vicksburg Daily Commercial. December 31, 1881. Mississippi Department of Archives and History, Jackson.

Vicksburg Weekly Herald. June 24, 1861. Mississippi Department of Archives and History, Jackson.

Vicksburg Weekly Whig. December 14, 1859. Mississippi Department of Archives and History, Jackson.

PETITIONS

Petition to the Mississippi Legislature (to allow Jordan Chavis to remain in Mississippi). Record Group 47, Series 2370, Box 14, 128. Mississippi Department of Archives and History, Jackson.

PROBATE COURT RECORDS

Aquilla Quick. Marlboro County Estates, Apt 8, package 15, Aquilla Quick, micro-film C1612. South Carolina Archives, Columbia.

Jordan Chavis. Warren County Probate Court Number 2841 and Number 3444. Mississippi Department of Archives and History, Jackson.

TAX RECORDS

Claiborne County, Mississippi. Tax Rolls, 1820–1841, Box 3621. Familysearch.com.

Jefferson County, Mississippi. Tax Rolls, Box 3667. Familysearch.com.

Warren County, Mississippi. Tax Rolls, 1850, Box 29678. Mississippi State Archives, Jackson, Various Records, 1820–1951, and Familysearch.com.

Warren County, Mississippi. List of Insolvent and Delinquent Taxes for the Fiscal Year Ending May, 1871. Series 341/Box 3887/B2/R9/B8/51 (Jordan and Washington Chavis). Mississippi Department of Archives and History, Jackson.

Warren County, Mississippi. List of Errors, Insolvent and Delinquent Tax Payers, Warren County, Mississippi for the Fiscal Year Ending May A. D. 1868. Insolvent, Delinquent, and Other Tax Lists, Series 341, Box 30043, B1/R34/B3/S1 (Preston Chavis). Mississippi Department of Archives and History, Jackson.

Index of Names